Living Life in Growing Orbits

52 Weeks to Wholeness

Living Life in Growing Orbits

52 Weeks to Wholeness

Wayne C. Allen

2015

© 2015 Wayne C. Allen

Wayne C. Allen

Title: Living Life in Growing Orbits

ISBN 978-0-9877192-7-0

All rights reserved. No part of this book may be reproduced or utilized in any form, or by any means, mechanical or electronic, including photocopying, recording or by any information storage or retrieval system, without written permission from the publisher.

The Phoenix Centre Press

324-55 Northfield Drive East

Waterloo, On N2K3T6

The title of this book is taken from a poem by Rainer Maria Rilke

I Live My Life
I live my life in growing orbits,
which move out over the things of the world.
Perhaps I can never achieve the last,
but that will be my attempt.

I am circling around God, around the ancient tower,
and I have been circling for a thousand years,
and I still don't know if I am a falcon, or a storm, or a great song.

Dedication

This book is dedicated to Darbella MacNaughton, my life partner, friend, lover, teacher – she listens to me, shakes her head, laughs, and keeps signing on for another "year."

Also, to my mom and dad, Erma and Chuck Allen. May they rest in peace, as I certainly gave them no rest while they were living.

About Wayne C. Allen

Wayne C. Allen is the web's Simple Zen Guy.

Wayne was born in Buffalo, New York in January of 1951.

His interest in psychology led him to Elmhurst Illinois, where he completed a B. A. in (1973).

He immigrated to Ontario, Canada in 1975.

Wayne received a Master's in Pastoral Counselling (M.Th.) in 1983, from Wilfrid Laurier University, Waterloo, Ontario. Wayne retired in 2013, after 31 years as a psychotherapist. He is the author of several books, all counselling / Zen related.

Wayne's approach to writing, life, and living comes from his love of Zen. His emphasis is on living in the now, and taking full responsibility for "how everything goes." His books are written in easy to understand language, and his insights are fresh and to the point. Wayne emphasizes wholeness, peace, and clarity of thought.

You can read more at Amazon, or at Wayne's publishing site, The Phoenix Centre Press.

(http://www.phoenixcentrepress.com)

In his spare time he's a painter and photographer.

Wayne and Darbella are now travelling the world, teaching, learning, and enjoying "retirement."

Table of Contents

INTRODUCTION TO THE 2015 EDITION I

INTRODUCTION TO THE 2008 EDITION II

INTRODUCTION..III

ROCK—WEEK 1..1

WATER—WEEK 2...6

RAIN—WEEK 3 11

DROUGHT—WEEK 4... 15

EMPTINESS—WEEK 5.. 19

FULLNESS—WEEK 6...23

PASSION—WEEK 7...28

BOREDOM—WEEK 8 32

SORROW—WEEK 9 35

ECSTASY—WEEK 10 39

CLARITY—WEEK 11 42

CLOUDS—WEEK 12 46

CERTAINTY—WEEK 13 50

MYSTERY—WEEK 14 55

HOPE—WEEK 15 59

DESPAIR—WEEK 16 63

SENSUALITY—WEEK 17 67

SEXUALITY—WEEK 18.. 71

SILENCE—WEEK 19 75

SHARING—WEEK 20.. 79

FOCUS—WEEK 21 83

DIFFUSION—WEEK 22 87

TOUCH—WEEK 23 91

ALOOFNESS—WEEK 24 94

TRUST—WEEK 25 98

MISTRUST—WEEK 26 102

YOUR BODY—WEEK 27 107

YOUR MIND—WEEK 28..112

YOUR SPIRIT—WEEK 29 116

LOVE AND YOUR HEART—WEEK 30 121

FAITH—WEEK 31 126

FEAR—WEEK 32 130

GOOD BEHAVIOUR—WEEK 33 134

BAD BEHAVIOUR—WEEK 34 139

DARKNESS—WEEK 35 143

LIGHT—WEEK 36 148

THE MIDDLE WAY—WEEK 37 153

THE REACTIVE MIND—WEEK 38 158

THE RESPONSIVE MIND—WEEK 39 163

CONTROL—WEEK 40 168

RIGIDITY—WEEK 41 173

FLEXIBILITY—WEEK 42 178

BALANCE—WEEK 43 182

FLOW—WEEK 44 186

MASTERY—WEEK 45 190

THE ARCHER'S BOW—WEEK 46 195

PATIENCE – MAKING TEA—WEEK 47 200

DESTINY—WEEK 48 205

VOCATION—WEEK 49 208

WHOLENESS—WEEK 50 213

SERVANTHOOD—WEEK 51 218

ENLIGHTENMENT—WEEK 52 222

ROCK 226

EPILOGUE 227

ALSO BY WAYNE C. ALLEN: 228

Introduction to the 2015 Edition

I guess you could say that the book in your hands is the result of our endless moments in Costa Rica. As you'll see from the other Introductions, this is the third revision of this project.

2015 was a banner year for sales for the last revision of *Living Life in Growing Orbits*, and that's interesting, because this book has only been available from http://www.phoenixcentrepress.com, our publishing website.

That was solely due to my decision to format the book for a full, 8.5 x 11 page, making it awkward to publish as a paperback on Amazon, and impossible, (due to the old, table format) to publish as an ebook.

Anyway, I was sitting at the rancho, talking about my books with a new friend, and began to idly wonder what this book would be like with a "regular" format—6 x 9—to match the rest of our books.

And then I thought that some rewrites might make the content clearer.

In other words, I came up with a *project*, as sitting around watching the breeze move the water in the pool apparently wasn't enough for me.

I like this book, so I'm even hoping this will be a fun edit!

Introduction to the 2008 Edition

While I was writing my 2005 book *This Endless Moment*, a couple of my editors made requests for exercises, so they could experiment with what I was writing about.

I resisted for a bit—then I gave in, and included a group of exercises in *This Endless Moment*, as well as creating a small, downloadable handout with another 20 projects.

I think I resisted because I'd written *Living Life in Growing Orbits* in 1998, and it's nothing but exercises. Then I realized that it had never been polished and really needed work.

So, in 2008, I decided to have another look at *Living Life in Growing Orbits*.

Readers who followed through with the exercises reported that they "got" what I continually talk about. The only real problem I could detect was that the layout was a bit odd, and some of the writing needed punching up, or clarification.

So, I did a re-write and redesign of the book. While the book is still quite close to its 1998 "parent" version, there are subtle changes to the language and presentation.

I hope you will like the revision, and will gain much from following along, day-by-day, for the next year.

Introduction

Wholeness is an ephemeral thing. For most people, it seems to be an unreachable goal, something best discussed as a philosophical concept as opposed to an achievable reality. Given the continuing effort that moving toward wholeness entails, most people choose to settle for "average." And the world suffers because of this choice.

You have decided to find an alternative to *average*, to *settling*, to *simply getting by*. Over the next 52 weeks, you will have opportunities to think deeply, to focus both inward and outward, to evaluate your choices, and to broaden your horizons.

I would not, for a moment, suggest that this work will be easy. There will be moments when you will feel like giving up, putting this book aside, thinking, "This may work for other people, but not for me." Let me assure you, this is a normal, even predictable response.

When this happens, stop. Allow the feelings associated with stopping the process to wash over you. Then, write them down. Think about them. Notice what story you are telling yourself—how you are stopping yourself. Read the chapter, "Making Tea." In the *pause*, as the drama dials back, clarity will occur, and you will choose to continue.

Working your way through this book represents a new beginning on a life-long journey. If you are wise, you will repeat this reflective process, in some form or another, for the rest of your life. This is either a delightful challenge or not, depending upon your perspective.

As to the way this book *works*: Each week is a separate chapter and begins with a thought for the week. These *thought pages* might suggest some form of writing, observing, or data gathering. You then turn to the *day pages*. Each day contains a "Word from Uncle Wayne," and a "Task for the Day." Both are intended to keep you focused, moving along, and aware.

It is not enough to simply read along. You must *actively participate*, both by doing each activity, and by writing.

To get the most benefit from *Living Life in Growing Orbits*, you will need a **workbook**—an additional pad of paper or a spiral notebook.

Use those blank pages to work through the questions raised in the 'thought for the week.' You will also write in your own workbook as the daily tasks dictate.

Let us begin, then, by simply being open to the possibility of a shift in direction. Let us walk together, with our eyes, ears, and minds open, available, and present.

There is no greater challenge than beginning

Rock—Week 1

Rock is the firm footing upon which we build our world. If possible we dig foundations to *bedrock*, so the things we build have the best chance of staying upright.

Rigid foundations necessarily resist movement—and it is the same with foundational *thoughts*.

Little children know nothing of the world. Adults and "tribes" teach the children what each tribe decides they need to know. These culturally accepted lessons of life, which each of us learn at others' knees, become our *foundational truths*, and help us to establish a firm footing in the world. In a sense, without such teachings we would be autistic. We would exist, but we would not be able to define ourselves or place ourselves.

The foundational truths we learn are, however, *subjective*[1]. Even more important, we have likely forgotten that we totally accepted, and are governed by, those foundational truths. They are that deeply embedded.

Foundational beliefs affect, as does nothing else, our *world-view*. A bald example: a divorced mother tells her daughter, age three, "Never trust a man. They'll all leave you." This one statement has the potential to colour all future relationships the young child has. And that's just one statement.

Of course, you will see the problem here. We incorporated these "truths" because, when we were small, *big* people (who had power or authority over us) demanded that we structure our being and behaviour according to these "truths." We incorporated them into our being, and they

---

[1] Subjective - one's personal (or a group's) experience of a situation, chosen arbitrarily out of all of the data available. Thus, foundational truths are not "true." They are accepted as "true" in order to support a pre-conceived belief.

have framed how we understand reality from that point on.

Unfortunately, however, some of these "truths" are non-helpful, or non-functional. We must begin by raising such "truths" to consciousness. Then, we can evaluate them more objectively—in a sense deciding if they actually work.

Make a list of all of the foundational truths you know about yourself and the world. As a hint, think about broad categories of things. For example,

- Think of people of different nationalities or races. What comes immediately to mind?
- What are your "truths" about men? Women?
- Business?
- Religion?
- Political parties?

Carry on from there.

Day 1
A Word from Uncle Wayne:
What you *believe* you were told dictates who you are.

Look at the list you just wrote. Do any of the "truths" seem to be causing you harm?

Often, we feel guilty for violating such a truth, even though we are not sure why we believe it. Think about the *result* of each belief you listed. **Find those with *negative* results**. Circle it or them.

Day 2
A Word from Uncle Wayne:
Reality Bites. Or not.

A *guiding principle* is your most basic principle. It directs who you think you are, and how you behave in the world.

Which item on the list is your guiding principle? (If you did not write it down on the first go, do it now.) Mark it "Guiding Principle."

Day 3
A Word from Uncle Wayne:
What would your life be like if you *chose?*

Define yourself according to your guiding "truths." Complete this sentence: "According to what I have been told, I am: …"

Day 4
A Word from Uncle Wayne:
No one knows you like *you* know you.

Using your best "parenting" or "helping" skills, give yourself a *brand new*, helpful, healing, guiding "truth." Complete this sentence: "If I were to choose to be whole, I would be: …"

Day 5
A Word from Uncle Wayne:
Not everyone (including members of your family of origin) has your best interests at heart.

Some (all?) of the items on your list of "truths" may now appear to be false. List a reason or two that people might have told you an "untruth."

Day 6
A Word from Uncle Wayne:
A wise old fish once said, "Learn to spit out the hook. Then, learn not to bite in the first place."

How do you continue to hook yourself with your "untruths?" Think of someone important in your life. Write down how you proceed from a disagreement with that person to being "hooked," and then to acting in ways *that never work*—that make the situation worse.

Day 7
A Word from Uncle Wayne:
With understanding comes both freedom and responsibility.

What would happen if you committed yourself to choosing to change the rules you live by? Remember, if you do, that you are entering the "scary unknown." What, do you imagine, is the worst thing that can happen?

Water—Week 2

Water is a major life force of nature and of us. We are mostly water, jostling around in the permeable shells of our bodies. We are not as solid as we seem.

Water, which seems so *insubstantial*, is powerful enough to cut through rock. That is where canyons come from. It doesn't seem to matter how hard the rock is. Hard rocks get water in their tiny fissures. The water freezes, the rock cracks. The simple flow of water dissolves soft rocks. A forceful water current does not stop. It simply goes around the rock, leaving it there, surrounded by water.

This week, we explore *water stories*. Water stories are alternative ways of looking at things—which eat away at our rock-like foundational statements. *Water stories* challenge your view of reality—your *rock* beliefs.

Water *experiences* are situations that come out differently than you might have predicted. Water stories describe those times when a foundational story you tell yourself about yourself and about the world no longer "held firm."

Here is a water story:

I worked with a client who had a *rock* belief that no one had ever complimented her. She learned this belief from her father, who taught her (*Rock story*) that there was nothing about her worth complementing.

One day, a man held the door for her and complimented her on her coat. She *heard* the complement. By the next week, she not only was hearing complements all the time, she was remembering back, and discovering complements from her past.

Remind yourself of one of your water stories. Remember

one time—or two—when the "predictable" was turned upside down, and you saw yourself and your world in a different light.

Day 1
A Word from Uncle Wayne:
Only do what works.

A water story changes the way we view something. This typically jars our system a bit or a lot, depending upon how deeply we held the view that "went away." Never minimize a water story.

Look again at *your* water story. As you change it from a "once in a lifetime, chance thing, of no importance" to "another, better 'truth,'" how do you feel?

Day 2
A Word from Uncle Wayne:
Listen more, talk less.

The wise person is thinking, "If I have one foundational belief that was shaken and went away, maybe I have more." You will see that many of your beliefs made sense to the person who taught them to you, but for you, they are untrue truths. Think about your untrue truths. Whose voice do you hear?

Listen to your water story. Whose voice do you hear? Listen for that voice in other situations.

Day 3
A Word from Uncle Wayne:
Toss a pebble—see the ripples, not the splash.

If you were to apply the truth of your water story's situation to your *life*, what would happen? How would you change? How would your relationships change?

Day 4
A Word from Uncle Wayne:
There are *excuses* for everything.
They mean *nothing*.

You have had the opportunity to explore and re-design a deeply held belief. So, you may be wondering, why don't I do this all the time? You don't because we all *make excuses*. You let yourself off the hook by coming up with a reason not to shift what isn't working.

What are your favourite excuses for not shifting?

Day 5
A Word from Uncle Wayne:
Don't leap. Take one step. Then another.

Now, without making an excuse, remember your water story. Play with the idea that this story has a *truth* that you can use in *other situations*.

Now, pick one other situation. Let the water story play with this situation. How does the story change? What small shift can you make to begin *living* your water story in this situation?

Day 6
A Word from Uncle Wayne:
It is easier to paddle with the current than to paddle upstream.

Most people, when making shifts, say, "It's difficult." This is an excuse to take forever to act differently. We do this to buffer ourselves against failure.

As you read this, you have *already decided* how long *your* shifts will take. So, admit it. How long will it take you to make the changes you want to make in your life?

Day 7
A Word from Uncle Wayne:
What you choose to "see" — you will be.

Write a slogan for the shift you want to make. Plaster it on the mirror you use each morning to get ready for the day. Then, actually read your slogan, every day.

Rain—Week 3

Most rivers are fed by *rain*. Rain is essential for the growth of all living things. If the rains fail, we have a drought and things begin to shrivel up and die.

Raindrops resemble the drop of water dripping from a tap. One drop and one drop and one drop. In isolation, a drop of rain is a small thing. We sometimes watch single drops of rain as they run across windowpanes. They chart a course and leave a trail, and yet we judge that they have no *impact*. Often, we ignore them.

They do get our attention when they bunch up, though. Suddenly, there is a cloudburst and you can no longer see through the window—or your clothes are soaked, and the fields flood and water is everywhere.

Truth is like a drop of water. It comes to us in small doses, from friends, enemies, out of a clear blue sky. If we notice, it leaves a trail, we see its pattern, and we are enlivened and fed by the wisdom of its truth.

If we choose to ignore the drop, the cosmos is kind. More droplets come. More truth. More lessons. Harder and harder lessons—until they deluge us, and we finally realize that all of them are trying to tell us the *same* truth the single drop told.

What truth about yourself did you learn easily—a "one drop truth?" What truth took a deluge to get through your resistance? What truth are you avoiding—are you in danger of drowning in? (Please towel off before writing them down!)

Day 1
A Word from Uncle Wayne:
Want to stay stuck?
Practice selective deafness.

Because we like to think we control our world and ourselves, we *categorize* things. We categorize the truths we hear into true or false, good or bad.

Some expressions of truth are **easier** to hear. Example: some truths are easier to hear from a *colleague* than from a *spouse*. What new truths do you accept easily?

Day 2
A Word from Uncle Wayne:
Want to be stuck? Do the avoid - dance.

Some truths are **hard** to hear. Our backs go up. We refuse to see what is going on. We freeze. We rebel. In short, we go into avoidance mode and nothing changes. What is your dance to avoid hearing, acting, changing?

Day 3
A Word from Uncle Wayne:
No one, by *thinking* about it, ever changed the course of a river.

Many people assume they have gotten somewhere by *thinking* about shifting. Nope. A shift comes when we actually do something *differently*.

What is your favourite strategy for *not* acting upon new truths?

Day 4
A Word from Uncle Wayne:
Bumblebees cannot fly. Apparently, no one told this to the bees.

It is normal to excuse a behaviour by saying, "That's just the way I am. I can't help it. Shifting my behaviour is difficult. I've always been that way." Right—and bumblebees can't fly.

You *can* shift. You *choose* not to.

Look again at your water stories and simply notice that you *have* shifted in the past. Own one new truth today. Then list one thing about you that needs to shift.

Day 5
A Word from Uncle Wayne:
Stop thinking of reasons *not* to shift.

Now comes the interesting part. What would you be like *today* if you implemented the new truth you listed yesterday? Think about all of the ways you will stop yourself from shifting even this one thing. Write them down.

Day 6
A Word from Uncle Wayne:
You're *here*. You get *there* one step at a time.

Return to yesterday's musings. What would a *first step* be for implementing your new behaviour?

Begin implementing your shifted behaviour, In stages. List the first step, right now.

Day 7
A Word from Uncle Wayne:
You have a problem. You get angry about your problem. Now, you have two problems.

Avoid all excuses. Take the first step you looked at yesterday. Don't get angry, or defensive, or sad, or anything else. Just take a first step and see what happens. If you did this *yesterday*, good for you! Take *another* step today.

Drought—Week 4

Like rain, drought comes unbidden and un-requested. Times of drought are times of devastation. Crops whither, rivers run dry; the air fills with cloying, choking dust. Often, with the drought comes locusts and other seeds of destruction, and all seems very bleak.

It is during drought that the rainmakers arrive—dancing, praying, and doing jigs, hoping to shift things through *magic*. Yet, *despite* the theatrics and prayers, drought comes and drought goes—in its own time.

People, especially those far along the path to enlightenment, will tell you of their "dark night of the soul." This is a time of silence and seeming abandonment, when even the voice of inspiration (however you view this voice) is stilled—and you seem very, very alone. The Desert Fathers called it (naturally) Desert Time.

In the midst of this time, this spiritual *drought*, we only want it to be *over*.

Yet, if we are still, if we *accept* the silence, we hear something in its voice. We see that, far from bringing death, the scorching heat and dryness of drought brings new, transformed life.

Walk in a desert and you soon see that life abounds. New, different life, strange life, but life nonetheless.

Tell yourself about *your* desert times, when you seemed to be lost and alone, and all voices were silent. Did you simply survive, or did you find a brilliant understanding about *new* life? Describe what you learned.

Day 1
A Word from Uncle Wayne:
There is no such thing as a dead desert.

Have you noticed how much time you spend *avoiding* being alone with yourself? Listening to you? Exploring the depths…of you?

When was the last time you looked inside, past your exterior? Make a list of your three favourite ways to avoid being alone with yourself.

Day 2
A Word from Uncle Wayne:
When wet, most seek to be dry. When dry, most seek to be wet. The weather does not care.

Desert Times are *not* depressions. Depression is a *modest* indicator that your life is out of balance. You can use depression to explore the depths of who you are.

Depression points to what you are avoiding. What was your last depression *really* about?

Day 3
A Word from Uncle Wayne:
Ever notice you can't hide in a sauna?

The dark night of the soul strips you of all pretenses, and you feel very alone. Depression just seems *bleak*; the dark night leaves you naked and revealed.

What would you see if you were stripped of all of your pretenses?

Day 4
A Word from Uncle Wayne:
Most people who pray do so by whining about problems, then telling their god how to fix them.

The dark night comes at the *end* of a descent into our *selves*. It comes when we see that what we believed about ourselves—and the world—is untrue, *and* we have yet to find a new way of understanding and being.

The solution is not *escape*, but silent waiting. Prepare for *your* dark night; plan *a silent day*, soon.

Day 5
A Word from Uncle Wayne:
It is amazing how noisy silence is for most people.

Many times this year, I will suggest that you sit in silence and follow your breath. Don't make this difficult. Just sit quietly and follow your breath in and out. Say, internally, "in," then "out." If your mind wanders, be kind to yourself—just start again.

Day 6
A Word from Uncle Wayne:
Is it water, or is it a mirage?

Many "friends," when they see us sad or teary, rush in with *solutions* to stop us from being sad. Why? We make them uncomfortable and they want us to stop.

Real friends sit with us, and encourage us to go deeper.

Who has rescued you too early from your "soul" work? Who will simply "sit" with you?

Day 7
A Word from Uncle Wayne:
Focus on the *real* issue, not the surface one.

The thing we *think* is the problem is almost never the real issue. The real issue is deeper. Spend your life fixing the surface, and the house will fall down.

There is only *one* way—finding time for silence and solitude, on a regular basis, is the best way to do your work. Commit to establishing a schedule for both silence and solitude.

Emptiness—Week 5

Emptiness is different from the aloneness of drought. Drought implies a lack of something, whereas emptiness is a state of being. Emptiness is the substance that exists between things, the insubstantial beside the substantial, the formlessness that encircles form.

Notice how substantial, how *real* your body feels. Go ahead. Grab hold of yourself, and feel the *reality* of you.

Then, touch the furniture, the floor, and a rock.

Now, contemplate life at the molecular level. Imagine moving downward to the atomic and sub-atomic level.

What would you find there? Ninety-nine percent nothing. Space. Void. Emptiness. Interesting.

For the most part, we are composed of nothing. At the sub-atomic level, the space between nuclei and electrons is immense. It is like the distance between the sun and Pluto (the planet, not the dog.) All physical matter is, is vast space surrounding little specks of matter, which actually might be vibrations. Or strings.

To be empty is to enter *voluntarily* the vastness of nothing. It is a meditative moment when everything stops—all chatter, all movement, seemingly life itself. In that silence, we find unity with the power that enlivens us. In a flash of emptiness, we see eternity.

Have you ever opened yourself to emptiness? Describe it. Was it a fleeting moment? Do you go there often? What did you learn?

Day 1
A Word from Uncle Wayne:
If you want to move, be still.

Focus your attention—spend two minutes, several times today, *consciously* shifting your focus from one object to another. Name it, silently, as you focus on it.

If your mind begins to chatter, simply continue looking around your environment, naming things.

Day 2
A Word from Uncle Wayne:
When you are burning to speak, be quiet.

Use prayer for meditation. For those of no fixed faith, try "Bring peace." Say one word on the in breath, one on the out breath.

For Christians, "Lord, have mercy." "Lord" goes on the in breath, "have mercy" on the out breath. For Buddhists and others, say "Om" on the out breath, just air in on the in breath.

Day 3
A Word from Uncle Wayne:
When you are drawn to stop listening,
listen some more.

Visualize your favourite peaceful holiday destination. It needs to be remote, warm (at least comfortable!) and safe. (Beaches work well. Disneyland does not.) Design this place carefully, in your mind. Breathe. Focus only on the destination. Do this for at least fifteen minutes.

Day 4
A Word from Uncle Wayne:
Anger expressed at others is usually anger regretted.

We need to learn to *let go* of anger. To notice it and express it through a physical activity is perfect. To express it at *a person* is usually courting disaster.

Today, we learn to shift focus. Imagine something about which you are angry. Then, rapidly shift your imagination to someone you love. Hold their image in your mind.

Monitor your body. Find the place where you physically *feel* the love. Allow your consciousness to go there and stay, quietly, for a few minutes.

Day 5
A Word from Uncle Wayne:
Being empty of expectations gives you choice.

Today, as you walk around, as you meet people, notice that you have *expectations* about who they are and how they will act.

Your goal is to notice your expectations, yet not act on them, so you can hang out with the real person. Say to yourself (for example), "My significant other is exactly as she is, not as I want her to be."

Do this with everyone.

Day 6
A Word from Uncle Wayne:
Holding grudges only hurts the holder.

Think of one significant person in your life. Using a separate piece of paper, write all of the things you are mad at them for.

Empty yourself by burning the paper when finished.

Day 7
A Word from Uncle Wayne:
To be truly miserable, follow this advice:
Never forgive. Never forget.

Listen to your inner dialogue. As you catch yourself thinking something negative, mentally apologize to yourself and the intended victim. Then, have a breath.

Fullness—Week 6

In a sense, fullness contains everything. If a glass is full of water, the glass contains the oxygen and hydrogen molecules, as well as the emptiness that exists between the molecules.

We might say that fullness is that which encompasses emptiness, without fully defining it (because something is always outside of the fullness—in our illustration, the glass.)

The "fullness of time" describes a moment of completion, when all of the elements of creation conspire to create something wonderful.

We sense this when we are enveloped in our sensations, overwhelmed by the beauty of something. Think of an orchestra playing the fourth movement of Beethoven's Ninth Symphony, when the choir begins to sing. Imagine the huge trees on the West coast of Canada. Visualize an unbelievable sunset, the cry of a child, or the look in the eyes of your lover.

This is fullness. This is joy.

We use expressive language—a *riot* of colour, a *cacophony* of sound, a *brilliant* flash of light, to describe the feeling of being bowled over by fullness. It is as if the thing could not be any bigger without bursting.

Each such moment is part of the endless flow of time—the moment, and the experience, will pass. Clinging will not prolong fullness. It is, until it is not.

What are your moments of fullness like? Where do you feel them? What do you do with them? What is it like to walk on the edge of being overwhelmed?

Day 1
A Word from Uncle Wayne:
No one ever died from too much joy.

Did you know that smiling releases brain chemicals that make you happy? It's true. Doesn't that just make you want to smile? Do so today. They'll wonder what you're up to.

Day 2
A Word from Uncle Wayne:
Whatever people are doing must make them happy. Why else would they do it?

We all know people who *love* to be miserable. We can see them setting themselves up for another round of misery, then blindly ploughing ahead. Even when we point it out, they continue.

Now, what about you? What do you do to make yourself miserable? What names do you call yourself during the process?

Day 3
A Word from Uncle Wayne:
Savour the sweetness of life.

Often, we are in such a rush that we speed right past the sweetness and beauty of life. What do you do to find the time and the place to savour life? Slow down!

Day 4
A Word from Uncle Wayne:
Joy is best lived in this moment.

People think that their happiness is down the road (way, way down the road!), when everything is going to be *just right*. They do not allow themselves joy along the way, in the moment. Do you do this to you? If so, how?

Day 5
A Word from Uncle Wayne:
No one can make another person happy.

Another good one: "If only *you'd* change, I'd be happy." This is popular because, when they don't change, you have someone to blame for your misery.

Guilty of this one? What would it be like to let others off the hook?

Day 6
A Word from Uncle Wayne:
Bliss is where you find it.

How much "self-limiting" do you do? Many only give themselves permission to be happy in rare situations. Where do you "allow" yourself to be content, happy, ecstatic? How would it be to find bliss *everywhere*?

Day 7
A Word from Uncle Wayne:
Bliss builds.

What can you set in motion today that will feel good to accomplish, and also will bear fruit down the road?

Passion—Week 7

We need to expand our definition of passion.

We often think of passion in sexual terms, as something that "makes us" lose control: it happened "in the heat of passion." We're saying, "Something happened that *dominated* me, and I was out of my own control."

Passion has negative connotations. We describe some crimes, for example, in this way—as a "crime of passion." Again, the sense is of things "getting out of control."

Another usage occurs when we talk about someone *being* passionate. See? Your mind likely moved back to sex (and if it didn't, it did now!)

As we overcome the sexual drift of the mind yet again, we remember that people are passionate about the things that "turn them on." Could be their profession, their art, their hobby, music, writing, whatever.

How about this? *Passion* is the "fuel" that drives us to excel. It is the prime mover.

That said, how many passionate people do you know?

Most people seem curiously *flat*. Our socialization, and the stresses of life, seems to conspire to rob us of passion. Think about it—if someone is really animated about something, so animated that they seem to be bouncing up and down with excitement and joy, don't we want to step away from them? We want to holler, "Get a GRIP!"

We do this because we have learned to rein *ourselves* in. Passion is consuming. It is a fire in the belly. The world tells us *we* will be consumed by our passions. The world suggests dis-passionate thought, or another beer, another stupid TV show, a drug. Whatever. Just, please, please *stay in control.*

In truth, passion sets us free. Passion *can* devour us, but wouldn't you rather be devoured by something you love *ultimately* than to choose to be bored to death by being "just like everyone else?"

~~~

Passion is a *choice*. What do you remember of your passions as a child? As a teen (don't be shy—describe them—in all their drippy splendour!) What are your passions now? Make a list. What *might* they be, if you gave yourself total permission? Is there a common denominator?

Day 1
A Word from Uncle Wayne:
Passion is what passion *does.*

Passion is not real unless you *enact it*. In other words, passion that you only *think about* is selfish, unfulfilling, and ultimately damaging. Damaging because passion attracts us, and internal passion continually unexpressed leads to myopic introversion. What passions do you *enact*?

Day 2
A Word from Uncle Wayne:
Live in the moment, as that's all there is.

Passion is immediate. Our passion pulls us in. We feel its heat as we think about it, and then enact it. It captures our attention completely.

Write about the things that capture *your* attention.

Day 3
A Word from Uncle Wayne:
Stop starring in "The Night of the Living Dead."

Passion is created, and passions never die. They just keep getting pushed back until they seem to disappear. Nevertheless, they are there, aren't they?

Look at your list of things that used to "turn your crank." Write down all of your reasons *not* to do these things. Keep this list until tomorrow.

Day 4
A Word from Uncle Wayne:
Try laughing. It turns your face on.

Doesn't thinking about your passions make you want to giggle, or laugh? Well, go ahead. Get into it. And burn yesterday's list.

Day 5
A Word from Uncle Wayne:
Play a little game, and see what you learn.

Sit with a friend and defend something in your most excited, animated, exuberant voice. Then, trade roles. (Don't comment or criticize, just be enthusiastic.)

Day 6
A Word from Uncle Wayne:
Passion is a well-tended flame.

Notice how you dampen your enthusiasm. Think about why you do that. Do you really need such great control? Afraid of seeming foolish? Analyse why you do what you do to turn yourself off.

Day 7
A Word from Uncle Wayne:
Once a week, do something outrageous.

Make a list of things you could do that would raise one eyebrow on your best friend's face. Try one, and see what happens.

Boredom—Week 8

Boredom is the opposite of passion. Boredom comes in many guises. Being "refined." Polite. Adult. Focussed. Polished. Disinterested. Analytical. Scientific. These are some of the more palatable names given to a way of being that cannot, or will not, focus in on anything and treat it as if it is *important*.

Boredom kills relationships. It does not feel good when someone takes you for granted. There is a sense of pushing against nothing. The bored person is "missing in action."

Boredom destroys attention spans. When you think your life is boring, you cannot focus. This is why most people, according to the "Peter Principle" (remember that one?) rise to the level of their *incompetence*. Because they lack motivation and a sense of purpose, they "rise" to the point where, with minimal effort, they can *get by*.

Boredom means that you choose to *minimize* or *shut off* any channels of stimulation.

The world is the same for all of us. That I choose excitement for life is not a proof that my life is exciting and yours is not. It is a proof that I know how to find a cure for my boredom, and you choose not to.

How do you bore yourself? What things in your life do you declare to be boring? Have you ever escaped boredom? How?

Day 1
A Word from Uncle Wayne:
Be bored and the world is bored with you.

Your mood rubs off on the people around you. So, because we tend to see what we choose to see, we find that people appear to be how *we* are. For example, if you are bored, you will discover many bored looking people around you, and not notice those who aren't.

Try altering your face to mirror another mood, and see what happens.

Day 2
A Word from Uncle Wayne:
Learn to change your focus.

What do you normally look at? Some people focus on "life," as in, "My life sucks." Others focus on details, as in, "If only I was smarter, taller, thinner. Since I'm not, I'll be unhappy." Try bouncing your focus around. In. Out. Big. Small. Details. Patterns. Seek a focus that helps you to alleviate your boredom.

Day 3
A Word from Uncle Wayne:
Do the dumb stuff first.

What do you really bore yourself over, so much so that you leave it for last? Do it first.

Day 4
A Word from Uncle Wayne:
When in boredom land, get up and move.

Walk a little today, and see, really see, where you are walking. Keep focusing outward toward your surroundings, not inward into your head.

Day 5
A Word from Uncle Wayne:
Boredom is simply a bad habit.

Today, correct yourself, lovingly, each time you sigh and choose to bore yourself. Talk yourself into doing something different. See what works.

Day 6
A Word from Uncle Wayne:
Boredom only exists in a vacuum.

Have a boredom party. Invite three friends. Go around the circle, trying to convince the others that your life is more boring than their life is. Keep going, and do not let anyone else win. See how long you can stay bored.

Day 7
A Word from Uncle Wayne:
Build an anti-boredom account.

I've created images in my mind—happy, excited, passionate, funny, witty, etc. When I feel something I do not like, I pull out a mental image and review the negative thing's opposite. Then, I can shift my focus quite easily.

Create some of your own.

Sorrow—Week 9

Many people think of sorrow as "being sorry for" something. Whether or not I equate sorrow with blaming myself, sorrow is *thinking* about or *regretting* something that happened in the past. This, once said, seems obvious, but *in the midst* of sorrow, the sorrow seems immediate—very present and real.

The distinctions we make about what we are experiencing dictate the results of the feelings we have. What I mean is this: if sorrow is your *present* reality, and by sorrow you mean, "I feel guilty about" something, then that will be a different experience from sorrow over, say, the death of a friend. In neither case can we do anything to change what has happened. Nevertheless, the method of dealing with these two things is radically different.

Sorrow needs to be experienced gently and profoundly. Repressing sorrow is a sure recipe for disaster.

The way out? We need to do what we need to do. This means that our sorrow or grief response is intensely personal.

Sorrow for mistakes, misdeeds, and missteps—again this is a human response. To be human is to fail. To be *fully* human is to attempt to repair the damage we do. To waste time feeling bad by endlessly rehashing the past is the ultimate waste of time.

Fix what you can, and let the rest go. Let's look at how.

How do you handle sorrow? What things do you regularly trouble yourself about? How many of them can actually be changed?

Day 1
A Word from Uncle Wayne:
Sorrow is often the absence of *peace*.

Experiment today with gently touching the issues that you sorrow yourself over. Seek to understand each issue from other perspectives. What do you do to keep your sorrow controlled, as opposed to experiencing it?

Day 2
A Word from Uncle Wayne:
Unresolved sorrow looms larger and larger.

How do you deal with things you sorrow yourself over? Ignore them? Dwell on them? Attempt to repress them?

Picture your "sorrow style." Write down what do you do.

Day 3
A Word from Uncle Wayne:
Often, the cure for sorrow is an apology.

If we act hastily and without thought, we make mistakes. Most simply *obsess* about the mistake, and then figure out a way to blame themselves *and* the other person.

Think of such a situation in your life. Now, imagine what might have happened if you had *immediately* apologized… then picture doing it in a way that works.

Day 4
A Word from Uncle Wayne:
Sorrow needs a limit.

Grief and sorrow need expression, but not *forever*. Many people continue to beat themselves up over things that happened *years* ago.

Think of as many things as you can that you regularly mull over with sorrow. Date the events. Are any more than a week or two old? Write after the older ones: "Can't do anything about this one."

Day 5
A Word from Uncle Wayne:
Events have a pattern.

Look back over yesterday's list. Any patterns? Common people? Common situations? This is proof that we tend to repeat behaviour that does not work. List the kinds of things you do that you *know* you will later regret.

Day 6
A Word from Uncle Wayne:
Think laterally.

We repeat non-helpful behaviours because we have never considered an *alternative*. Look at yesterday's list. Think laterally. List other, quite different behaviours or actions, ones that will get you better outcomes.

When (yes, when) one of the above patterns repeat, you will have thought of additional, more helpful behaviours. You will then "only" have to apply one.

Day 7
A Word from Uncle Wayne:
Learn to let go.

We tenaciously hold on to our obsessions. To shift this, we need to have this in mind: "I am holding the thing I am obsessing about in my hand. I am setting it down and walking away from it. I allow my emotions to lift as the distance increases."

Ecstasy—Week 10

Ecstasy is one of those things people think they are looking for, and would prefer to have "it" all the time.

I like to think of ecstasy as a "peak moment" or "peak experience," which is not the same thing.

People who climb mountains do not ordinarily remain on the summit. This is mainly because life is difficult to maintain up there, but actually, were you to stay, soon the top of the mountain would seem boring. *Anything* becomes boring if you are "in it" for too long.

Most people know this, but try to hold on to each ecstatic moment as long as possible, milking from it the last drop. Others resist having ecstatic moments at all, fearing the pain they think they will feel when it ends.

In both cases, people miss the point. These moments are there to savour just as they are—as a glistening experience of joy, celebration, and renewal. It's not about holding on, or avoiding. It is about enjoying each situation in its moment—and savouring its memory when it ends.

Ecstasy is not a *goal*. It is a state of being that is both a reward and a blessing. Ecstasy does **not** come so that we might see how good life *could be*, but rather so we notice how good life *is.*

Ecstatic *moments* are signposts along the way. They are to be entered into unreservedly, experienced and appreciated, and then left behind as the walk of life continues. This receiving and letting go allows us to take the energy of the ecstasy with us, rather than being obsessed and possessed by it.

What is ecstasy for *you*? How do you experience it?

Day 1
A Word from Uncle Wayne:
From the mountain-top, you can see where you came from, *and* where you are going.

Write a list of four or five profound, ecstatic moments you have had. Review and relive them. Notice the power they still have, and the lift of energy they provide.

Day 2
A Word from Uncle Wayne:
Each moment contains a lesson, if we look and see.

What were the *lessons* in each of these moments? Did they tell you something about yourself, about your walk, about the world?

Day 3
A Word from Uncle Wayne:
Moments of bliss allow us to glimpse perfection.

Ecstasy provides clarity. We see through *things* to the inner rhythm and perfection of life. However, many begin to judge the process. How do you *remove* the wonder and perfection from your ecstatic moments?

Day 4
A Word from Uncle Wayne:
Ecstasy is all around us, as close as breath.

Some think they have to go someplace high up or exotic to find breath-taking ecstasy. They are right. Because they *believe* this, they cannot see or experience ecstasy *except* under the conditions they have set. They therefore miss the ecstasy at their feet. What conditions do *you* put on ecstasy?

Day 5
A Word from Uncle Wayne:
Be open to the moment.

On the other hand, you can have ecstatic moments in quite mundane settings. Think of the most "common" ecstatic moment you have had lately, where something or someone touched you deeply. List it.

Day 6
A Word from Uncle Wayne:
Life is best lived with wide-eyed wonder.

Open your eyes today. Force yourself to look, to see, to hear. Stay centered and focused, with your spirit open and receptive. Anything *interesting* happen?

Day 7
A Word from Uncle Wayne:
What you *want* is what you get.

Try thinking that everyone and everything is connected. *Everything affects everything*. The only thing that keeps you stuck is your belief system.

Try this: say, "For this moment, I'm open. I will see beneath the surface to the truth of things."

Clarity—Week 11

Yesterday's (and last week's) work prepared you to take two weeks to wrestle with clarity and clouds. Clarity is what happens on the mountaintop (when there are no clouds, of course!)

Clarity is a focus thing. If, for example, you have ever used binoculars, you know about focus. Each time you turn your attention to a new thing, assuming it is at a different distance from you, you have to refocus the binoculars. If you do not, you cannot see clearly.

So, how often do you refocus *your life*?

The thing that keeps us from seeing clearly is our worldview. It works like this. Something is painful. Rather than simply *facing* the painful *situation*, we search around for someone to blame. We pick someone. From that point on, all we see, when with that person, is what we have already decided we will see.

Example: Someone yells at you. Instead of stepping back, looking at the situation, and finding creative ways to resolving things, you either get mad at the other person, or blame yourself. These approaches lack clarity.

On the other hand, you will remember instances where you have suddenly found yourself looking at things in another way; there is relief and closure.

I want to suggest to you that *choosing* clarity—seeing in a way that *resolves* issues—is always possible. Whether or not you do this is, as usual, entirely up to you.

※※※

This time, write a list of instances you remember when something confusing simply "cleared up." How did *that* happen?

Day 1
A Word from Uncle Wayne:
It is *you*, not them.

Imagine—your best friend sees you, and turns away. You try to talk. She snarls, "Leave me alone! You have never understood! I want to be alone, and you are in my face. When I need you, you're not there." She bursts into tears and walks away.

Write a story. What just happened?

Day 2
A Word from Uncle Wayne:
Clarity comes as you focus away from what leads to darkness.

Here is some new information to add to yesterday's story. Your best friend had just received a phone call from her mother, telling her that her grandmother had died. Change anything?

Day 3
A Word from Uncle Wayne:
Clarity comes from understanding.

Often, there is more to something than the "obvious." This is why it is so important to slow down and get more information before popping off in some dumb direction.

List three ways to slow down your need to "fix things" or "punish."

Day 4
A Word from Uncle Wayne:
Take responsibility for your own clarity.

People with clarity know *themselves,* and are responsible for making elegant choices about situations. They find intelligent ways to deal with others, and positive approaches for dealing with themselves.

Think of three things you could say to yourself to bring yourself into clarity.

Day 5
A Word from Uncle Wayne:
Let go of what does not work.

Using binoculars without changing the focus would not be a clever thing to do. Yet, often, we get into a pattern of behaviour that gets us predictably bad results, and yet we repeat it.

How many dumb behaviours do *you* repeat? List them.

Day 6
A Word from Uncle Wayne:
Focus on what works.

To be whole, we must learn to focus on what works, as opposed to what does not. Most of us know what we do *wrong*—less so, what we do right.

Think of recent situations where you figured out what was *really* happening. How did you do that?

Day 7
A Word from Uncle Wayne:
Clarity, at its base, is *in*sight.

Life is best lived from the "self" (or centre) outward. Otherwise, we think we are buffeted by the winds of fate. Phooey. Go inside. See yourself in relation to the situation you face. Look for several different responses. Notice that with choice, comes *understanding*.

Clouds—Week 12

Clouds block the view.

You are standing on the mountaintop, and a sign, three feet away, (which you can barely make out,) tells you that: "You can see Three Rivers from here."

Right. Nothing but white fog.

Internal clouds are pre-conceived notions. We set up an understanding, usually involving blaming our misery on ourselves or someone else. The result is sadness, inability to act, and despair. Clouds of our own making.

The key theme of this book is that each individual is responsible for how he or she perceives reality. Absolutely no one on the planet "makes" you do (or be) *anything*.

Out of all the choices available to you, you choose a single response. If you are wise, you choose ways of being that bring healing and peace, for you and for others.

Unfortunately, it is much more likely that you have devised a series of understandings that keep you stuck, unable to see alternatives. Clouds.

This book, at its best, is about helping you to see in new ways. The first step is to acknowledge destructive patterns.

So, guess what? It is time to list yours. What are the clouds in your life? What do you believe about yourself, and others, that keeps you stuck?

Day 1
A Word from Uncle Wayne:
When you are stuck up to your knees in the mud, no matter what else you think, they are *your* feet, and you walked there.

Most people are aware of, and can describe, the things they do, repeatedly, to avoid paying attention to "where they are." And *suddenly* they are in trouble. In other words, you already know how you repeatedly end up in the same swamp. List your repetitive behaviours.

Day 2
A Word from Uncle Wayne:
Responsibility = "I am *able* to respond differently."

Look at yesterday's list. Ask yourself if you are telling yourself that there is something about your behaviour(s) you *cannot* change. That's a cloud. Write it down. Any more?

Day 3
A Word from Uncle Wayne:
All shifts start with choice.

If you *think* you can't, you can't. Doesn't mean you *really* can't. It really means you "won't."

Look at yesterday's list. Take a guess here: how do *other people* make shifts that keep them from doing what you are doing?

Day 4
A Word from Uncle Wayne:
Find a "life coach."

This book is a life coach of sorts, but wise people are everywhere, if you look. Pick something you think you should shift, but "can't." Think of two people you could talk to, and ask them what they do in a similar situation.

Day 5
A Word from Uncle Wayne:
Reward your successes. Correct your mistakes.

This, briefly, is the mark of wisdom. Wise people do not dwell on their mistakes. They make *corrections*. They repeat what works, and are always looking for ways to live life even more elegantly.

Wise people are *not* perfect. They are just more flexible. List five ways *you* could be more flexible.

Day 6
A Word from Uncle Wayne:
Stretch yourself. You will grow.

Pick another cloud issue and spend the day thinking about alternative behaviours. Make as long a list as possible, without judging the list.

Day 7
A Word from Uncle Wayne:
Eventually, the sun breaks through.

Clouds are not solid. We can make them long lasting, but they do not *have* to be. Promise yourself, today, that you will actually deal with the clouds remaining in your life by *implementing* the shifts you wrote down yesterday.

Certainty—Week 13

Being a former Yank, I have imbedded in my mind the first words of the Declaration of Independence, "We hold these truths to be self-evident..." As I get older, I wonder—what truths, exactly, *are* self-evident? Is it limited, as the adage says, to "death and taxes?" What is human dignity worth, these days? Apart from a few general principles, what do you hold to be self-evident? To whom?

As we move from the world of science to the world of inter and intra-personal dynamics, we seem to think that surely there must be as much "certainty" in our psychic lives as in the "real" world.

Now, of course, no one would argue against the truth that we need oxygen to breathe. It is a "death and taxes" truth. No air—you die. When we get to "meaning of life" questions, things become more complex.

As we *clearly* view life, the more obvious it becomes that there are multiple realities, each "right" on some level, or at least "correct" to some group or individual.

This is not an easy lesson to accept. As we involve ourselves in the lives of others, of course we hope that their worldview will match ours (and if not, we hope we can *change* their worldview!)

The mark of maturity is the ability to understand and empathize with multiple worldviews.

In the end, the only certainty seems to be that we *are*. We exist, occupy space, and create a worldview. From this comes the corollary that reality is subjective.

How long is your list of "certainties?" (Ignore the physical world ones, i.e., gravity, etc.) What rules motivate you, especially in the direction of anger toward others who "break" your rules?

Day 1
A Word from Uncle Wayne:
The world is exactly as you perceive it.

Take an issue you feel strongly about. List it. Defend your position.

Day 2
A Word from Uncle Wayne:
There is always another viewpoint.

Hold up your hand, palm toward you. You can see your fingerprints. Someone opposite you sees your nails (Are they clean? (I digress…)) Which is the *correct* view?

Take yesterday's issue. Argue an opposing view with as much intensity as your own view. (Remember, we are *playing* here.)

Day 3
A Word from Uncle Wayne:
You do not have to accept another's point of view as your own. It is foolishness, however, not to *acknowledge* it.

Truth is relative, at least at the interpersonal and intrapersonal level. We never have to *agree* with a divergent opinion. We need to understand that others hold their views with equal conviction. We can agree to disagree. Just listen, today, for divergent views. Stop yourself from judging the other person. Just listen.

Day 4
A Word from Uncle Wayne:
A non-helpful goal: make everyone think like me.
A helpful goal: be curious about how others think.

To change *others* is an impossible task. To do your best to see another's perspective is to have the freedom to reach understanding, to shift your own position, or to agree to disagree.

Think about an issue you have with another person. Identify the rule you hold that the other person is violating. In the end, is your rule *enforceable*?

Day 5
A Word from Uncle Wayne:
Limit your certainties.

Return to this week's idea page and look at the list of things about which you need to feel certain. See if you can reduce the list to five items or less.

Day 6
A Word from Uncle Wayne:
Be certain about *yourself*.

One of my friends was mad at a person who called him a liar. I asked my friend if he *was* a liar. He said no. He also said the other person had no right to call him a liar. Yet, he *had* called him a liar. Do you see the ambiguity—the problems looming on the horizon? Life is not about getting everyone to vote in our favour.

Day 7
A Word from Uncle Wayne:
Ask yourself, "What can *I* do?"

The pronoun that you choose to govern your life by is key to being centered and self-responsible.

Listen to yourself today. What percent of your pronouns are "I" and what percentage are "you"? The only ones that matter are the "I's."

Mystery—Week 14

I spent much of the Spring of 1996 exploring several issues in my life, with the help of my therapist. At the fifth session, she said that she thought I was past my issues and doing fine. She then asked, "Do you understand what caused this thing, or how you got out of it?"

I said that I was not sure.

She asked me how that was for me. I said I did not like it. I said that I would really like to *know* what happened.

She replied, "Kind of hard *not to know*—to accept that life is simply a mystery we never really understand, eh?"

I laughed, and had to agree. She smiled and said, "Good. Now spend six months actively not knowing."

I did. I'm still doing it (thinking and saying, "I don't know…") and it is *still* difficult.

Of course, we want to know "why," "how," "what's happening." We figure that if we can *understand* life, we can *control* it. That would be nice, I guess, but it simply "don't work like that."

We never get to figure life out. We may get a piece of it, or an insight into an issue, but the "next one" will be sufficiently unlike the "last one" as to need a new approach.

Life, then, is best lived by those who can cope with mystery.

The cosmos is designed to teach us the lessons we do not know that we need to learn. If we seek "certainty" (see last week's topic) we will live a life of disappointment. If, on the other hand, we can learn to treat life as a riddle to *explore*, as opposed to *solving* (there is a difference) we have the best chance of maintaining balance.

How does the mystery of life sit with you? What stories do you tell yourself when you think about sitting quietly in the midst of "not knowing?"

Day 1
A Word from Uncle Wayne:
Mysteries are fun when they are not ours.

We want things to be stable and predictable. Life is seldom either, so we tilt against life, trying to make it cooperate.

What does the word "mystery" set off in you?

Day 2
A Word from Uncle Wayne:
Enter into the mystery.

It seems paradoxical, but in order to be successful at life, you have to *enter* the mystery, becoming involved in it, as opposed to simply observing it.

List the themes in your life that you *wish* would change, but which you touch reluctantly, from a distance.

Day 3
A Word from Uncle Wayne:
It's not the solution, it's the process.

In movie mysteries, the detective always solves the case. In real life, it is often about simply being present as the mystery unfolds. The learning comes from watching ourselves interact with something difficult to explain.

How is this for you?

Day 4
A Word from Uncle Wayne:
Mysteries drive us deeper.

Superficial solutions always involve either trying to make *others* change, or minimizing the importance of the issue.

Think about the ways you shift responsibility or minimize the issues in your life. List them.

Day 5
A Word from Uncle Wayne:
Mysteries are best appreciated in the depth.

Remember, it's not about *solving* things. It *is* about noticing the patterns, the dilemmas, the weave of our lives, and how certain themes keep cropping up in new guises. List a few of yours.

Day 6
A Word from Uncle Wayne: Be quiet!

We have been here before. Simply focus on one of your issues or mysteries, and do nothing but observe it. What happens?

Day 7
A Word from Uncle Wayne:
You cannot take a mystery seriously.

Mystery requires a light touch, or it gets away from us. Entering the mystery is like catching butterflies. Again, reflect on one of yours, but try to hold it, and you, gently.

Hope—Week 15

Hope can be defined by using the familiar cliché, "This too shall pass."

Hope is a state of awareness that understands that nothing is fixed or permanent. All things change. Hope-full living actively encourages a change for the better.

Many times, we distract ourselves with the *situations* we find ourselves in—and find that we *lose* hope. The language here is quite precise. Hope is easily lost, misplaced, and forgotten. Why? Because a "hope-less" situation brings with it a morbid fascination.

Have you ever noticed that, when you trouble yourself over something, there is a sensation that the situation is drawing you into *itself*—into the darkness, drama, and pain, and soon you can see nothing else? It is difficult, at that moment, to be hope-full.

Hope is the belief that life and situations *shift*. Why would we ever be motivated to leave our bed of sorrows, if not for hope? Hope is also the understanding that things can change in a direction we choose to go in. Hope motivates us to tackle difficult things. As such, you might think of hope as being "a single-minded focus in a positive and purposeful direction."

What things do you hope to change during our year together? As you look at what hope *knows*, how do you see yourself? Who will you be as you make the changes necessary in your life?

Day 1
A Word from Uncle Wayne:
Hope tells us what *could* be.

Hope is forward-directed—toward what we want to bring into being in our lives—toward what we wish to see in the lives of others, and in the world.

List a few of your hopes for others, and for the world.

Day 2
A Word from Uncle Wayne:
Hope is a habit.

It is easy to be hopeful about life when nothing is wrong. To have hope in the midst of despair—that is tricky.

How often, actually, do you feel hopeful? How do you *discount* hope?

Day 3
A Word from Uncle Wayne:
Ungrounded hope is fantasy.

Discipline is required for us to learn to walk through life moment-by-moment. From a practical perspective, most people set huge goals, expect to get there in one step, and are disappointed.

Look at the lists of things you hope for. What would be the *first step* to accomplish each of them?

Day 4
A Word from Uncle Wayne:
Hope's sister is patience.

The greatest destroyer of hope is impatience. Once we figure something out, we want all of the results *now*. As I noted yesterday, most things do not happen that way.

Write a couple of sentences about *your* patience level.

Day 5
A Word from Uncle Wayne:
Let life gently unfold.

We need to learn to watch, gently prune our thoughts, and softly nudge ourselves along the path hope suggests. Life is lived while walking through change, not after the change is over.

Think of a time where you gently observed an event, appreciating each stage of its unfolding. Easy? Hard?

Day 6
A Word from Uncle Wayne:
It is the journey, not the destination.

To be hopeful is to be observant of the walk itself.

People *lose* hope either because they don't accomplish what they've hoped for, or because they *do* accomplish it and are disappointed with the results. In the latter case, they only focused on the destination; they missed the joy of the walk. Then, they discover there is no "there" and there's more walking to do.

What did you actually *do* today to fulfil your hope(s)?

Day 7
A Word from Uncle Wayne:
Hope is the tour guide to *This Endless Moment*[2].

Be gentle with yourself today. Review your hopes, your steps along the way, and thank God for where you are. That would be "sufficient for the day."

---

[2] Bit of a joke here. *This Endless Moment* is the name of my most popular book! So, have you read it?? You can read about it at www.phoenixcentrepress.com

Despair—Week 16

Anybody out there who has not felt the cold, clammy hands of despair creeping up their spines? Despair is a voice that reminds us of our failures, real or imagined. Mostly imagined, as it turns out.

Despair is a sneaky head-trip that manages to find a fatal flaw in everything about us. Of course, once the period of despair is over, we can clearly see that not many of the negative things we said about ourselves were of much use. We see how we could have thought that way, we just cannot figure out why we would have *wanted* to.

We wanted to because we have been trained to *blame*. Despair is self-blame, writ large. If only I had different parents, more skills, straight hair, whatever. We immediately begin to do two things: absolutize and awfulize.

Absolutizing is making everything either / or. I am the *worst* person. *Everything* is wrong. *Nothing* is going right. The more we use absolutizing language the "truer" we perceive it to be. Our sub-conscious mind wants to provide us with what we ask for. If we ask our sub-conscious mind to prove we are awful, it will do so, *simply by ignoring any evidence to the contrary.*

Awfulizing: This is where we take the stuff that is happening and describe it in the worst possible light. "The way he's looking at me must mean he hates me." "This situation can only get worse." "There is no hope."

How do you awfulize and absolutize? What words do you use? Are you good at it? (You will know you are if, as you talk to yourself, you usually make yourself feel worse.)

Day 1
A Word from Uncle Wayne:
It is as awful as it seems to you.

Get this into your head: everything that happens to you is subject to your interpretation. The "spin" you put on it determines how you see it, feel it, and understand it. Despairing thoughts are specifically designed to make you feel worse. They serve no other purpose.

What is your favourite reason for despair?

Day 2
A Word from Uncle Wayne:
We can convince ourselves of anything.

I once had a couple in for therapy. She eventually left the marriage because he did not polish the kitchen taps often enough, and to her, that meant he did not love her. Nothing I did could convince her otherwise.

What do you believe about you, and about others, that causes you pain?

Day 3
A Word from Uncle Wayne:
We write the stories of our lives.

Stuff happens. We put the spin or twist on the events. That is why one person calls an experience a "failure," and another person calls the same thing a "learning experience." Guess which person is most likely to have an attitude that will get them where they wish to go.

What is the theme of the story of your life?

Day 4
A Word from Uncle Wayne:
It takes effort to have a life.

Many people sit and stew in despair because that is what they have *always* done. They tell themselves that they are powerless to stop it. And guess what? They are!

What, about yourself, do you tell yourself you have no control over?

Day 5
A Word from Uncle Wayne:
Give yourself a shake.

You stop despair by aggressively challenging its conclusions, while listening respectfully to its messages. That little voice in your head is *never* going to go away, but you can choose to direct your mind to challenge its conclusions. The process of self-examination and the re-creation of hope is a *discipline*.

Look at your list of despairing comments to yourself, what would be corrective sentences for each of them?

Day 6
A Word from Uncle Wayne:
Despair loses strength in light.

Shine some light on your despair. Go out. Listen to music. Write. Talk to a therapist. Do something. Don't sit and wallow.

What has worked for you in the past? Write it down!

Day 7
A Word from Uncle Wayne:
Vow to do the best you possibly can. Then do it.

Treat yourself with gentle discipline, and remind yourself that you are *living* your life, not just going along for the ride.

What does the idea of gentle discipline mean for you? How can you be of support for yourself? More focused? More aware?

Sensuality—Week 17

We move, for a few weeks, from our minds to our bodies—which is sort of a funny thing to say, as changes in how we understand our bodies are made in our heads. That is why this is a journey into *wholeness*, as opposed to a journey into fragmentation.

We have a disconcerting habit of saying *"sensual"* while thinking about sex. Sensuality is often reduced to something like foreplay.

Sensuality unpacks as "expressing what one's senses sense." I use the word "sensuality" to describe "fully and completely feeling our feelings—our sensory inputs."

A young woman, in describing a symphony concert, wrote, "It's like the sound dances around your heart, pulling at all your emotions and saying "be part of the music..." The sound surrounds you, consuming your whole body... It's a feeling of excitement and joy."

Sensuality means allowing yourself to deeply feel what you are sensing. Music *overwhelms* you. A work of art or a beautiful mountain floods your eyes and *erupts* in your brain. A chocolate-covered strawberry *explodes* in your mouth.

This is Sensuality.

We desperately need to learn to let go and be in the flow. We need to learn to totally release ourselves into excitement and joy, and come back out, renewed.

※※※

List the best experiences you ever had with your eyes, ears, mouth, nose, and skin.

Day 1
A Word from Uncle Wayne:
We can find, in everything and everyone, overwhelming beauty.

Sensuality is about passion for life. The important part is learning to be open to being bowled over by the gifts of life.

Look at your list from yesterday. Describe your feelings regarding your sense-ual experiences.

Day 2
A Word from Uncle Wayne:
Celebrate your body.

Give your body gifts. Play a piece of music that makes you bubble. Or cry. Eat a lemon. Go for a run. Take a bubble-bath. Bake an apple pie, smell it for a while, then eat a small piece, very slowly. Allow a piece of expensive chocolate melt in your mouth. (No chewing!) Give yourself a hug. Sing in the shower.

Day 3
A Word from Uncle Wayne:
Reach out and touch someone.

Many people avoid contact with other people—because we are incredibly bad at differentiating between sensuality and sexuality. We need to learn to touch again.

Feed someone your favourite fruit. Play music for someone. Give someone a hug. Reach out.

Day 4
A Word from Uncle Wayne:
Let's have a breakout of human kindness.

This Week's topic is about being gentle. It is about sharing the pulsing of wonder that is our world. Make a vow, right now. Give a gift, every day for 365 days. Suggestions: Write a note. Leave a flower. Give someone a perfect leaf. Offer to drive. Smile and say, "Boy, it's good to see you!"—and mean it. Wear a funny button. Tell a joke. Draw something and give it away.

Day 5
A Word from Uncle Wayne:
Always speak words of blessing.

Tell *yourself* something positive, every 15 minutes or so, either about yourself, or about the world around you. OPEN your eyes and ears!

Say something encouraging to someone. Offer to help. Never lecture. Always bless.

Day 6
A Word from Uncle Wayne:
Tune in.

We live life on autopilot, looking to confirm our own worst fears. We stop autopilot by *paying attention*. Paying attention is a sensory thing—get it? You have to listen, and see, and feel—then touch the world.

Hook into a method to come out of la-la land and notice what is happening. Cool, eh?

Day 7
A Word from Uncle Wayne:
Go play.

Stop being so serious all the time! Exert yourself. Find a sport—live, and breathe it. Take up an art form—express yourself. Push yourself. Set attainable goals, get off your butt, turn off the TV (external and internal), and go have some fun.

Sexuality—Week 18

We are sexual beings. We can't help it—we were created that way. We are different from everyone else on the planet, and we are attracted to those differences. We all crave closeness with someone outside of ourselves.

Sexuality, at its best, is a sharing of the depths of our selves. It is never possessive. That's why, when we are in a relationship that has no depth, sexual infidelity seems like the ultimate betrayal. You might not have a relationship, but at least you "own" your partner's body.

There is joy in sexuality, obviously. This, too, takes work. It involves knowing ourselves, what we need, what we like. It involves risking, asking, giving, and receiving. Sexuality requires endless openness.

Sexual *attraction* is also a given. It happens. The mature person learns to enjoy it while not *necessarily* acting on it. In the arena of sexuality, as in no other, it is essential to establish healthy boundaries.

You will see that, like all the other sections of this book, this topic takes thought, without making *excuses*. It is not about defending what you are doing. It *is* about carefully exploring your feelings and understandings about sex and sexual expression.

What are your "sexual rules"—your sexual do's and don'ts? What things (acts, rules, people, etc) do you confuse yourself over?

What do you find embarrassing, what would you experiment with, but are afraid to?

Day 1
A Word from Uncle Wayne:
Your sex organs do not have brains.
So, stop thinking with your genitals!

Have you ever acted out sexually when you "knew better," then regretted your decision after the fact?

Write about: How did you talk yourself into it?

Day 2
A Word from Uncle Wayne:
Figure out your body.

You need to know what makes you tick, sexually. This one gets interesting. Most people are afraid to ask what their partner wants or likes, and are afraid to ask to have their needs met.

To be sexually mature is to *easily* articulate your needs and ask your partner(s) about theirs. Can you?

Day 3
A Word from Uncle Wayne:
Write about your first sexual experience.

Funny how that first one can set up some strange beliefs. Good or bad, it likely was immature, but is still, somehow, influencing things.

Rather than being jerked around by it, explore it. Listen to how you describe it. What is the message? Write about it.

Day 4
A Word from Uncle Wayne:
Learn to like yourself.

Healthy sexuality is a part of a healthy self-image. You have to know and *like* your body, mind, and spirit.

Start here: Look at yourself in the mirror, naked, and then have a pep talk with yourself. Say kind things. Move from your body to mind and spirit.

Day 5
A Word from Uncle Wayne:
Live your fantasies.

Think of a sexual fantasy. Or ten. Are any of them possible? Likely.

Write them down, then tell a partner / friend. Figure out how to make it / them happen. Then trade off and do one of his or hers.

Day 6
A Word from Uncle Wayne:
Be a romantic.

Watch a great 40's movie. Learn how to dress, flirt—how to have a date, and how to talk. Sexuality is not simply coitus. It is the whole package. And non-coital romantic encounters are sexy, too.

Day 7
A Word from Uncle Wayne:
Sexual tension / attraction is real. Deal with it.

We tend to deny attraction, especially of the sexual variety, and especially if we are involved with someone else. Yet, the attraction is there, just under the surface, and we keep bumping into it.

In your primary relationship, talk about *what* attracts you to others, and, as far as you know yourself, *why*. This, of course, takes a strong relationship—but we would not have any other kind, would we?

Silence—Week 19

Whatever might "Silence is Golden" mean? Most of us (me too!) never come up for air. And those who choose not to do much physical talking often chatter endlessly in their heads.

Silence is learning to shut up, internally and externally. This section will give you some pointers.

In silence is wisdom. Answers arise in silence.

Silence can be scary. It is almost as if we fear that if we stop talking, or if our minds get quiet, we will die.

On the other hand, it is true that people who really know each other have the ability to be silent in each other's presence, and no one gets offended or rushes in with words to fill the gap.

Sometimes, silence is poorly used. Example: "If I do not speak, I cannot be wrong." Or, some think that if they don't ask, they will never be disappointed. "What would I do if I asked for something, and didn't get it?"

Silence can be a weapon. If you know that the other person is "tortured" by your silence, you, at some level, get to enjoy their pain.

This is *not* how we view silence. We are looking for the subtle silence that allows you to truly hear and see what is going on around you, without the need for continual interpretation. This form of silence simply observes. It is therefore a *meditative* process.

※※※

How do you feel about silence? Is it good, bad, indifferent, loved? What keeps you from creating more?

Day 1
A Word from Uncle Wayne:
Sometimes, simply being with someone is enough.

We often lead with our mouths. We say things we regret, or say things that do not help, or just speak to fill the silence.

Think about, then write about, a time when silence would have been the better choice.

Day 2
A Word from Uncle Wayne:
Follow your breath; feel your roots.

Finding space for silence is a discipline. You have to build times for silence into your daily routine.

One way to do this is to develop a breathing practice. Monitor the flow of your breath, in and out. Feel the breath in your nostrils, coming in, going out. As you breathe in, imagine the breath going down to your feet, and your feet "rooting" into the ground.

Day 3
A Word from Uncle Wayne: Bite your tongue!

Be conscious, today, of how much time you spend in your head, not listening to the person you are in conversation with, as you frame your response, or as you talk yourself out of talking.

Instead, try listening to the other person—really listening. Work toward understanding where the *other person* is coming from.

Day 4
A Word from Uncle Wayne:
Communicate non-verbally.

In our "touchy-feely is bad" world, we have stopped reaching out with anything but words. Yet, touch is calming, warming, comforting, and focussing.

Today, choose to communicate by holding someone's hand, or by giving him or her a hug.

What are other ways you could use touch effectively?

Day 5
A Word from Uncle Wayne:
Find a silence partner.

Suggest to a friend that the two of you spend 15 minutes together… in silence. Then, do it.

Day 6
A Word from Uncle Wayne:
Learn to look out of your eyes, into the eyes of another.

After doing yesterday's project, do this with your friend. Sit opposite your friend, and look into each other's eyes. Hold your gaze, without looking away, for a minute or so. This may be quite difficult.

If your partner is willing, keep at it by practicing regularly.

Day 7
A Word from Uncle Wayne:
Cultivate silent walking.

Go for a walk, and do nothing more than silently name the objects you pass. As your mind wanders, bring it back to "simply naming."

Sharing—Week 20

I like to think of sharing as "walking with." Sometimes it's about sharing your experiences with others, to give them another perspective to contemplate. Or, it's giving someone the gift that he or she *really* needs—your time and attention.

Sharing is *not* about grudgingly giving up your toys so others can play with them, despite what you were taught as a kid.

Sharing is the willingness to be an active participant in the life of another. To share is to be able to be *open* with another—to be directly involved in the ongoing saga of their life—to be deeply involved in their personal growth.

Sharing is best when there is balance or equality between the two people. Sometimes, however, a person will be in your life in a special capacity—as a teacher, guide, or therapist—and the balance will tip. Most *good* teachers will encourage you to restore the balance by teaching *others* what you are learning.

Remember that life is the *totality* of our activities. It is impossible to live life trying to be in a perfect sharing relationship with everyone else. It is certainly possible to live in a sharing, caring way *on average*.

❦

What are some of the things you share easily, and on a regular basis? What things do you share grudgingly? What (or who!) will you *never* share?

Day 1
A Word from Uncle Wayne:
"Teach" 10 others.

I once tried to thank my therapist for all she had taught me. She said, "Go teach 10 others, and ask them to do the same."

Notice who teaches you, and what. Teach others the best of what you learned. This is sharing without an ulterior motive, as the benefit accrues to *others*.

Day 2
A Word from Uncle Wayne:
Stop thinking anyone owes you anything.

What are some of the things you think "others" or "the world" owe you? Examples: Others *should* treat you in a certain way, or *should* speak to you using a certain tone of voice. Or, thinking that people should be grateful for "all you've done for them."

Make a list of your expectations.

Day 3
A Word from Uncle Wayne:
You *cannot* get your needs met by others.

Burn yesterday's list.

Day 4
A Word from Uncle Wayne:
Sharing is *voluntary* and without *motive*.

Commit to *continually* examining your motives and understandings concerning your relationships—especially the problematic ones.

Many times, what seems to be a misunderstanding is really a "crossed" set of expectations.

In most cases, the "cure" is a generous heart. What does that mean for you?

Day 5
A Word from Uncle Wayne:
Avoid manipulation.

Ask yourself this: do you ever do something with the expectation that the action will "make" another person change his or her behaviour toward you? Have you noticed that this never works?

Today, ask directly for what you want, and accept that you will either receive it, or you will not.

Day 6
A Word from Uncle Wayne:
Just hang out.

One of the most difficult things to do is to establish a relationship based upon *no* expectations, other than being fully engaged in what is happening *now*.

Think about that one. What would it be like?

Day 7
A Word from Uncle Wayne:
Share *time*.

Hanging out is being present, in the moment, and noticing that you are delighted to be where you *are*.

Is this something you do? If not, why not? How could you begin "just being?" Think of some specific times, places, and situations to do this.

Focus—Week 21

Focussing is one of life's most difficult tasks. It seems that everything is calling for our attention—people, the world, and that little voice, nattering away in our heads—because of this, we are very distracted.

In 1996, a major challenge occurred in my life. It was so profound that *everything* shifted. For the first two days, the pain of the challenge, the *unfairness*, was all I could focus on. I then realized that if I spent all my time obsessing about this situation, I was going to lose *myself*.

I brought my focus *away* from the issue and *toward* the present moment. I did this by focusing on my breath.

As I watched the inflow and outflow of breath, I noticed that my mind stilled, and in that stillness, the real issues came to the fore. I was able to deal with the crisis *in its time and as necessary*.

I suspect that this skill (and it is a skill, which requires *practice*) is not a common one. We are conditioned to gripe and moan and complain, thinking that the world is unfair. This is a mind-set.

We were taught—and continue to teach ourselves—to *obsess*. So, we need to learn that when our mind goes in some direction, we have a choice whether to follow—to continue with that train of thought.

The mind can be led to what is of *real* importance. We do this through the discipline of focus.

※※※

What is focus like for you? Easy? Difficult? Something you remember only after the crisis is over?

Day 1
A Word from Uncle Wayne:
It is never about what we think it is about.

Monitor your mind for a 30-minute period today. In order for this to work, you have to be gentle with yourself. Simply sit down with a pad of paper and a pencil, and do not *do* anything. See where your mind goes.

Write down a word or two about each place your mind went.

Day 2
A Word from Uncle Wayne:
Focus on your breath.

When we stress ourselves, we tend to hold our breath. Given that the principal "food" for the brain is oxygen, this is not a good thing.

Seems hard to believe that you have to *think* about breathing, but it is true nonetheless.

Concentrate today on breathing deeply and easily.

Day 3
A Word from Uncle Wayne:
Structure your obsessions.

We all obsess—we seem to *need* to obsess.

Set a timer for 15 minutes. Sit down and obsess sequentially through all the things that are bothering you. When the timer goes off, stop, get up, and do something else!

Day 4
A Word from Uncle Wayne:
Surround your obsession with goodness.

Many, when they obsess, choose *anger* as a reaction. This gets us nowhere, but it sure feels *righteous*. While it is a cliché, it is also true that *what goes around comes around*—we tend to get back the energy we put out.

It is not enough to try to avoid thinking about difficult situations. Today, visualize a stressful situation, then think of peace and healing.

Day 5
A Word from Uncle Wayne:
Anger is a good antidote to obsession.

Sounds like a contradiction, eh? Try it. Find a safe place. Lock the door. Internally or externally, "aim" your anger *toward a mental image* of the thing that you are angering yourself over. Do a good job. Set a timer for 15 minutes. This way, you are *in charge* of your obsession. This is the key to *focused* attention.

Day 6
A Word from Uncle Wayne:
Focus means being "in the zone."

Remember a situation when time seemed to stand still—when your productivity was incredibly high and your creative juices were flowing. That's "the zone."

Think back to your last trip to "the zone." What did it feel like? Remember that feeling.

Day 7
A Word from Uncle Wayne:
Focus on being focussed.

Focussing is not *easy*, or we would all be doing it. It has to be a *priority*, and only you can make it one.

How will you choose to make it a priority?

Diffusion—Week 22

Diffusion is the opposite of focus. It is the *absence* of focus. It is the state of non-focus. People in this state say, "I don't know what to do."

Diffusion is more *physically* draining than any other state, which seems to be a contradiction. Here is what happens: we "crave" *fulfilling our individual needs.*

According to Maslow's "Hierarchy of Needs," base issues of food and shelter are the primary focus. As we meet those basic needs, we then move further up the scale, where our needs become more sophisticated—all the way to the top, which Maslow called self-actualization.

At every stage of the game, however, there is the countervailing tendency to "freeze." We become confused, and are no longer willing to act.

This process, this shutting down, happens to everyone. We get to a point where we understand something—then our world shifts, we confront an obstacle to our continued progress, and we recognize that our present understandings are incomplete.

There are two possible reactions. We gain new understandings, or we enter into fear or frustration, and there we sit—frozen. In order to survive in this frozen state, we pull back into what I call *diffusion confusion.*

Diffusion, then, is the result of freezing—of fearing to go forward and afraid to go back.

What issue or issues are you presently "freezing" yourself over? How do you *do* diffusion?

Day 1
A Word from Uncle Wayne:
Stagnant water often smells.

Diffusion is more than being stuck. Being stuck means you are working on something and the answer has not occurred to you. Diffusion means *forgetting* you are stuck. You make excuses for doing nothing.

What excuses do you give power to? Write them down.

Day 2
A Word from Uncle Wayne:
Diffusion is atrophy at the core level.

We have a Core that is *home* to the life force that enlivens each of us. This force empowers us and helps us to "get" where we are going.

What does the idea of the Core mean to you?

Day 3
A Word from Uncle Wayne:
Stop making excuses for your life.

When we get into "diffusion confusion," we find ourselves in *neutral*, and neutral, perversely, often feels comfortable. Your life will go on if you live on autopilot. You just will not be of much *use*.

Devise a way, today, to ask yourself if you are diffusing.

Day 4
A Word from Uncle Wayne:
There is never a good diffusion.

Some diffuse on holidays or after a trauma. I remember a holiday in Venezuela, and meeting a Corrections Officer who was on holiday, and was *totally shut down.* Talk about autopilot. He was not even on the planet. In his diffusion, he missed the beauty of the place.

Review your list from day one of this section. Think of other ways you diffuse.

Day 5
A Word from Uncle Wayne:
Lean on nothing.

Whom do you depend on to "fix" your crises, diffusion, and problems? How come *they* were elected? We all need assistance occasionally—guidance, counselling. But propping up? Forget it!

Write on a poster: Lean on Nothing and No One.

Day 6
A Word from Uncle Wayne:
Take possession of your channel chunker.

I owe Darbella for that term. Channel chunkers are TV remote controls.

You have a million channels of input. Diffusion is choosing the one channel that is nothing but snow and fixating on it—so, change the channel!

Make a list of things that really grab your attention. Put the list where you can find it and use it to restore your focus the next time you are tempted to diffuse.

Day 7
A Word from Uncle Wayne: Diffused people get hurt.

Diffused people walk into holes, real and imagined. You can depend on this: every time you "got caught" by something, you had tuned out, and didn't see it coming, or you diffused and talked yourself out of avoiding dealing with "it."

The solution, as usual: *Wake up!*

Touch—Week 23

Most of us remember the studies done some decades ago, where children in orphanages had one of two experiences. Kids in one group were touched and cuddled. The other group of kids received just enough touch to sustain life. The first group thrived. The second group defined the term *"failure to thrive."*

We communicate through touch. We need to recognize, however, that not all people communicate in the same way, and this applies to touch, too.

Because touch is so easily misunderstood, our society is moving in the direction of touch *avoidance*. A reassuring pat on the arm—a hug—have slowly become suspect behaviours. Some actually believe that *any* touch is inappropriate.

What to do? I suggest finding friends and setting "touch boundaries." Of course, this requires communication and maturity, things we are in short supply of in our society, but hey, this is important!

Then, there is self-touch, which is also important. Pleasuring ourselves is usually a code phrase for sexual stimulation. I would like to suggest the broader view.

We need to feel free to touch ourselves, to take long bubble baths, to use massage oil; in short, get to know our bodies. Sounds like interesting homework, eh?

What does the word *touch* bring up for you? Who touches you, and how? Whom do you touch, and how? How do you touch yourself?

Day 1
A Word from Uncle Wayne:
You ARE Your Body.

We tend to think that our "selves" reside in our heads, observing. Great. So, step outside your body. Tough, eh? "You" may be up there in your head, but you *are* emphatically also your body.

Pay attention to your body today—to its messages.

Day 2
A Word from Uncle Wayne:
Find three people to hug. Do so daily.

Hugs are the lifeblood of... life.

It would be good if you could find three people to hug per day **apart from** family members, but find three.

- Discuss hugging parameters so that each is comfortable.
- At least one person must be the same sex as you. (As several men throw down the book...)

Day 3
A Word from Uncle Wayne:
Life has its touching moments.

Write down five ways you like to be touched, but which are not happening. (It might be good to make two lists of five—one sexual, one non-sexual.)

Why is it that your five favourites are not happening? What can you do to set up ways to experience your five?

Day 4
A Word from Uncle Wayne:
Get yourself into hot water.

We have a hot tub. We talk. We invite friends for soaks. Hot water feels good. Another option—a hot bath, with essential oils, calms the senses. Try it, today.

Day 5
A Word from Uncle Wayne:
The medium is the *massage*.

One of the best ways to experience touch is through massage. Find a professional nearby and book an hour.

Take home what you experience, and share it with your significant other, and/or your friends.

Day 6
A Word from Uncle Wayne:
Some people are simply "out of touch."

Today is observation day. Notice how people touch, or avoid touch. Simply focus, and watch.

Day 7
A Word from Uncle Wayne:
It's like your friends say— "Keep in touch."

Notice how YOU avoid touch. Make a vow to be more open to the possibility of controlling your urge to *escape*. Recognize that, with good communication, touch becomes an excellent channel for making contact.

Aloofness—Week 24

Maybe I am imagining it, but being aloof seems to be a learned behaviour. I suspect what happens is that we extend ourselves, *be* ourselves, and someone criticizes us or takes advantage of us—or so it seems.

We *react* to this perceived rejection by putting up the wall of aloofness. We feign disinterest. We may actually *be* disinterested. We are, of course, present *physically*, but mentally and spiritually we are staring at life as if through a self-created translucent wall or barrier.

Now, of course, some might argue that given the way the world is, this is the only way to stay *safe*. There may even be some truth to that thought. Problem is, safe is *safe*. You never get to your growing edges when safety is primary. You protect, guard, erect barriers, shut down, and close off, and soon, you are living in a small space, and there is nothing happening.

The alternative is to recognize just how destructive being closed off is. As we recognise it, we can do something about it, without seeing ourselves as vulnerable. We can then choose to make contact.

Ask someone close to you to describe the ways you act when you are being aloof.

Day 1
A Word from Uncle Wayne:
People do what they do.
You choose whether to hurt yourself over it.

Now, this is important.

- Kids can be hurt by adults.
- People with weapons (or fists, etc.) can hurt you.
- You *cannot* be hurt by the words and actions (other than actual violence) of others.

You choose to react as if you're hurt, and that's a cop out: shifting the responsibility for your life off onto someone else. Stop running away or feigning aloofness!

Make a list of "hurts." See them another way.

Day 2
A Word from Uncle Wayne:
Aloof people are zombies.

Review and add to yesterday's list—*how* do you "do" aloof?

In what *situations* do you "do" aloof? Example: I "do it" at cocktail parties (which I avoid, mostly).

With whom are you aloof?

Day 3
A Word from Uncle Wayne:
No shifts come from being aloof.

Pick a significant other in your life. Do you "do" aloof with that person, perhaps as a way of "punishing them?" Does punishing someone ever get you what you really want? Does it ever bring you closer?

Day 4
A Word from Uncle Wayne:
Aloof is not cool.

No matter what the media says, aloof sucks. The problem is that the media represents aloofness as both *normal* and *cool.*

This "works" because being stuck in neutral *seems* better than pain.

The alternative is to learn to work *through* your pain, as opposed to opting for numb.

If aloofness seems cool, change your mental image. Replace the cool person with a zombie.

Day 5
A Word from Uncle Wayne:
The cure for aloofness is reaching out.

Pick someone, and open up to him or her, just a bit. Tell them how you *really* are.

Day 6
A Word from Uncle Wayne:
Snap out of it!

Find a way today to equate aloofness with tuning out. In other words, stop giving yourself permission to be stuck. Pinch yourself and *wake up*.

Day 7
A Word from Uncle Wayne:
Air out your head by opening your mind.

Ask for feedback from one person today. Ask them to let you know when you tune out or are acting aloof. Have them step on your toe or something. (I guess a gentle word in your ear would work just as well!)

Trust—Week 25

Trust is different from being naïve. Trust is a point of view or life-perspective that describes your *base line comfort level.*

Every person is somewhere on the trust <–> paranoia continuum. You think the world is fundamentally a safe place, and that "the world" can be trusted, or you do not. You believe people, overall, can be trusted, or you do not.

Being naïve, on the other hand, is walking around in a Pollyanna-like daze, stumbling into messes, all the while believing the songs the cartoon bluebirds are singing as they gently fly around your head.

To trust is to understand that things happen, sometimes for a reason, sometimes for no reason. Life simply *is,* and *the way it is, is the way it is.*

To trust is to understand that each of us is here for a reason, even if that reason is not immediately apparent.

To trust is to believe that you meet exactly the right people at exactly the right time—and that all people and situations are lessons to be experienced.

To trust is to understand that no one is out to get you—indeed, that you cannot be "got" without your permission.

To trust is to live fully and wholly, honestly and vulnerably in the world without pretending to understand how the world works.

How trusting are you? Write about your levels of trust.

Day 1
A Word from Uncle Wayne:
Trust involves the heart AND the brain.

Whom do *you* trust? Make a list. Are there areas of exclusion ("I certainly can't tell her *that!*") What do you fantasize would happen if you trusted more?

Day 2
A Word from Uncle Wayne:
Trust is an act of love.

Trust is about openness and sharing. Whom do you trust more—those you love, those you like, or those with whom you are merely acquainted? Why?

Day 3
A Word from Uncle Wayne:
Trust requires vulnerability.

Trusting is letting someone in on your biggest secret—who you are, and what is important to you.

To trust is to become *vulnerable*—at the very least to the possibility of someone betraying your trust.

The only way to never experience this "vulnerability / betrayal" dilemma is to *never* reveal yourself—not, in my opinion, a good choice.

Today, play with your vulnerability by asking, "What's the worst thing that could happen?"

Day 4
A Word from Uncle Wayne:
Just because you cannot trust *everyone* doesn't mean you can't trust *anyone*.

Eventually, someone you trust *will* burn you. It's not a question of "whether." It's a question of "when." Then what?

You must choose whether to risk trusting someone else. You can choose to mourn the loss of the former friend and then re-engage with another friend, or, you can live your remaining time without trust and vulnerability.

For me, the choice is obvious.

Make a short list of one or two people with whom to deepen and extend your vulnerability.

Day 5
A Word from Uncle Wayne:
Trust, like wine, needs maturity.

If you say, "People should treat me better," you are in for a bumpy ride through life.

Today, observe the interactions of people around you. Some interactions seem supportive, others, not so much. Notice that everyone is treated well by some, badly by others.

The wise person, when treated badly, trusts anyway, by not shutting down.

Day 6
A Word from Uncle Wayne:
Trust is a willingness to share your essence.

Today would be a good day to write a paragraph or two about who you are, really, at this moment.

Day 7
A Word from Uncle Wayne:
Build upon your past success.

What things, discovered yesterday, seem to be permanent parts of who you are? Which things seem to fluctuate? What would it be like to share with someone, at a deep level, only the permanent parts, just for "a while?"

Mistrust—Week 26

We are born trusting others. We become mistrustful through the experience of not having our needs met. The first instance of mistrust goes back to infancy, and to our first missed feeding, and "betrayals" continue until we die.

We trust someone, and then we judge that he or she has betrayed us. We react as if it never happened before, and we vow it will never happen again. And, of course, it does.

Like it or not, the rest of the world is not here to treat us *fairly*. Most people never figure out that they are, and always will be, essentially *alone*.

Everyone is "wired" to be self-focussed. People do *consider* us as they make decisions. Our good friends, with their deeper concern for us, are a great blessing, but to *depend upon* that friendship and concern to get our needs met is to court disaster.

To recognise why we mistrust, we have to understand that the betrayal of a friend seems much worse than the betrayal of an acquaintance. That seems obvious, right?

The problem is that we assume that when we trust someone, that trust is forever and unconditional. As opposed to the view that there are no guarantees, and that, given a peculiar set of circumstances, even the best of friends sometimes violate our trust.

If we can reach the point of *maturity*, we recognize that such betrayals are choices, (and is thus about the person who made the choice to betray) and there is nothing we can do about the behaviour of our friend.

How we choose to *respond* to the violation is completely under our control.

As usual, the question is not about why our friend did what they did. The question is, "What will I do the next time the world is not fair?"

Day 1
A Word from Uncle Wayne:
Life is not fair. It is just *life*.

What are your fairness rules? Have the words, "It's not fair?" ever escaped your lips? What happened, the last time?

Day 2
A Word from Uncle Wayne:
No one is coming.

This motto hangs on the office wall of my Therapist. It is the conclusion to the story of the person who expects rescue from the "White Knight" or God, or Jeeezus, or someone. The punch line is: "No one is coming."

Who (or what) are you waiting for, so that your life finally becomes OK?

Day 3
A Word from Uncle Wayne:
People have exactly as much power over you as you give them.

This flies in the face of the "victim mentality" so prevalent today. Everyone is looking for someone to blame for his or her misery. Parents. Bosses. The system. The distress we feel, however, is simply *ours*. The question is, "Given this situation, what will you do?"

List a few behaviours to use to take back *self*-control, the next time you think you are being victimized.

Day 4
A Word from Uncle Wayne:
People who look over their shoulder often run into walls.

The posture of someone locked into betrayal is "Walking forward, slowly, looking back." Or worse—"Standing still, looking back." Walls hurt when you walk into them, especially if you did not see it coming.

How often are you so caught up in examining past betrayals, so caught up in being mistrustful, that you miss the present moment?

Day 5
A Word from Uncle Wayne:
Learn from mistakes, and then move on.

That is what mistakes are there for, remember? What lessons have you learned from past violations of trust?

Day 6
A Word from Uncle Wayne:
"Positive Thinking" is Stupid.
Clear Thinking Rules.

Blow off the slogans. Enlightenment does not come from sloppy, sophomoric aphorisms. Wisdom is about understanding that no one is here to make your walk easier. Wisdom comes from overcoming obstacles.

Those who violate your trust are *also* your best teachers. Weird world, eh?

What betrayal was your best teacher? What did you learn?

Day 7
A Word from Uncle Wayne:
Be Real.

Have your feelings, willingly. Stop yelling at yourself. Listen to the voices of your inner theatre. Then, choose your next path. Where do you need to go—where have you been "too busy" to go?

Your Body—Week 27

The Eastern view works for me—we are Spirit (Chi, Qi) *fully* residing in bodies. Bodies are containers for "us," but are not a "thing"—we do not own our bodies—they *are* us.

We can use them, but we cannot preserve them—just like our cars, they are rusting and wearing out even as you read this line. Thus, if you identify *only* with your body, you are doomed.

Our bodies feel. Our bodies provide data and stimulus—we see, touch, hear, etc. only as our bodies send signals to our brains. Our bodies give us boundaries (and a sense of self) and help us to differentiate between "inside and outside." Our bodies attract some people and repel others.

In the West, we live under the thrall of the Cult of the Body, which is part of the Cult of Eternal Youth. We spend billions trying to reverse the ageing process—one of the things that is natural to our bodies—without spending two cents studying the connection between Mind, Body and Spirit.

The Western Church, starting with Augustine, taught that we are born in sin, that feelings (especially sexual ones) are unclean, and that *suppressing* the body is the goal of the religious person.

If we are to survive, we must destroy this belief system and discount any institution promoting it.

In order for our Spirits to learn, we have to interact with others. I am not sure of any reliable methods for interacting with another, other than through our bodies. We have to talk, to listen, to see, to touch (you can also smell and taste, but not so easily in public!)

Most Western bodies are sensory deprived, and as we move more and more into a "don't touch" mentality, we wonder why we feel so cut off. To disembody ourselves in response seems to me to be the height of stupidity.

As a first step, we need to learn to nourish and care for our bodies. How do you feel about your body? Do you recognize that you *are* your body? So you know that you are *more* than your body?

Day 1
A Word from Uncle Wayne:
Learn to love what you've got.

Stand naked in front of a full-length mirror. Look at yourself. Figure out a way to see your back. Look for those things about your body that you *like*. Express your positive feelings out loud. (This is possibly the hardest exercise in this book!)

Day 2
A Word from Uncle Wayne:
Make friends with your body.

Head back to the mirror. Examine areas you are less pleased with. Ask yourself, "Do I dislike this part of me because it is truly unhealthy, or am I judging myself on the basis of Hollywood and magazine ads?"

Recognise that most of us look *average*, and that is OK. Say something kind to a body part you have been angry with.

Day 3
A Word from Uncle Wayne:
Exchange meaningful compliments with someone you care about.

Make a pact with one or two significant others (preferably one male, one female) to make positive body comments. "I really like your ears," "You have strong hands," and "I respect the wise lines around your eyes," is what I have in mind.

Day 4
A Word from Uncle Wayne:
Don't compare.

Look at your friends as embodied Spirit moving through life. You can appreciate what you find attractive about their bodies, and understand that they have as much trouble with their body as you do with yours. Be kind, both to them and to you. Don't compare.

Day 5
A Word from Uncle Wayne:
Speak kindly to yourself. After all, you *are* listening.

Find ways to compliment your body aloud. Just like day 3, but speak aloud.

Day 6
A Word from Uncle Wayne:
Be nice to your body.

Touch yourself. Massage yourself. Recognize that your body is yours to play with, caress, and make love to and with. It is yours. Give your body a hand—so to speak.

Day 7
A Word from Uncle Wayne:
Don't forget yourself.

In your favourite workspace, place a picture of yourself. Dar and I do a photo calendar, featuring us, every year, and hang it in the kitchen. You could do a more "interesting one" and hang it in the bedroom. Put your favourite picture of *yourself* on your desk, along with the other ones. It will remind you of who you are, this incarnation.

Your Mind—Week 28

With the Enlightenment came the supposed supremacy of the mind over the body, and the Spirit became the sole (grinning...) property of the church.

Scientists became our priests and, and they assumed that *reason* would solve all of our dilemmas.

Western Scientists decided that the way to understand anything was to break things down into their component parts. The theory went that at the root, base (particular, molecular, atomic, and sub-atomic) level, everything would become clear.

The joke of the 21st century is that, as we have broken things down, things have broken down. At the sub-atomic level, we find space, space and more space. In a sense, everything is mostly nothing. Yet, our minds, conditioned by three centuries of scientific research, cannot let go of the idea that we are smart enough to understand what is going on.

Your mind is a wonderful thing, if used as is intended. It is a storehouse of experiences and data, and is great at creating categories and clever strategies. The myth is that, with enough information, your mind can *understand*. Nope. Your mind simply apprehends, stores data, and makes suppositions (tells stories.)

Many people spend their lives in the "If only I knew why 'this' happened, then I would be happy" place. Natter, natter, and natter. No wonder we are in a mess.

❧❦❧

Our goal is to be at peace. To be whole. What would it be like, to vow to never "know anything" for sure?

Day 1
A Word from Uncle Wayne:
Learn to laugh at your mind.

Re-mind yourself that you are in the "real world" only when you are *out of your mind*. (Take that any way you want!)

What happens in your mind is not *real*. Your mind reasons, solves math problems, and reminds you not to step in front of the approaching bus. Your mind reviews the past. Your mind does future planning. This is good, but remember—nothing ever works out as you plan it.

Today, get out of your mind. Say, "That's just my mind. It's not real." Then, just observe.

Day 2
A Word from Uncle Wayne:
Tell your mind to shut up.

Take a minute or two to observe where your mind goes. Just watch. Quietly, tell your mind to be calm.

Day 3
A Word from Uncle Wayne:
Give your mind a break.

Buy a book or go to Zen Centre, and learn to meditate. The silence will surprise you. You can actually turn off the mental voices for increasingly long periods. Practice!

Day 4
A Word from Uncle Wayne:
Listen non-judgmentally.

Refrain from ragging at yourself. The critic is a part of everyone's repertoire. For example, your internal critic says, "Hey! Stupid! Are you on about that again? Grow up!"

Quiet the internal critic by being kind to yourself. "Well, there we are, wool-gathering again. I wonder what's happening out in the 'real' world?"

Day 5
A Word from Uncle Wayne:
The mind, like a horse to water, can be led to good things. But will you drink?

The best way to counteract the mental critic is to change channels. Think about other, more interesting and fun thoughts—in fact, make a list. Then, when you start in on yourself, you'll have backup material to shift to.

Day 6
A Word from Uncle Wayne:
The conscious person's motto:
"I am always learning new things."

Each day gives you the opportunity to find something new to think about and act out. Each day, another thought can swim around in there, changing your perspective. This is a good thing.

If you do not direct your mind to new paths, you are destined to repeat the past. Be in charge. Learn something new.

Day 7
A Word from Uncle Wayne:
Seek only peace.

Meditation is also about *asking*. Condition your mind to ask "God," the cosmos, your higher self, for peace. Go into your mind, touch your Spirit, and say, "In this space, in this time, bring peace." See what happens.

Your Spirit—Week 29

Finally, you are home—yet, for most, the Spirit is an unexplored realm.

With the Enlightenment came a *diminishment* of the Spirit. Into a world where the Spirit had ruled for millennia, came the ascendancy of the mind.

The Spirit became the territory of the professional holy men, with the following twist. The Spirit ceased to be the most *important* realm. The mind was elevated, the Spirit relegated to an hour or two a week. Far from being the chief motivating element of life, Spirit became religion, and in the words of Karl Marx, the "opiate of the people."

Most people have trouble identifying their Spirit. Peak experiences, workshops, excellent teachers, all touch the Spirit, and body and mind are flushed through and through with peace and a sense of "Yes! This is how I should be!" For most, the flush wears off, and it is back to "life as usual," as they seek the next Spiritual high.

I would suggest that the Spirit has eyes, ears, and a voice. Spirit provides the alternative view. The language of your Spirit is odd—"Love your enemies and bless those who persecute you."

Spirit understands that we are *here*, on different paths, with different gifts, so Spirit does not seek uniformity. It promotes love and peace.

The Spirit senses irony and laughs. Spirit senses paradox and puzzles over the riddle. Spirit does not seek answers—Spirit lives with the questions. The Spirit, in short, is Zen.

The Spirit is the realm of light, fire, and wind. Spirit is the seat of passion, creativity, and wisdom. Spirit looks for itself in the eyes of others.

For most people, Spirit is undernourished and unappreciated. Yet, your Spirit also brought you to this book, and brought you to the path you are now walking.

The rest of this book is dedicated to strengthening your Spirit.

Now, have you talked with your Spirit lately? What did you learn?

Day 1
A Word from Uncle Wayne:
Listen to the wind.

"The Spirit blows where it wills." Nothing about Spirit is *predictable*. We expect it in dead rituals; mostly it is not there. We feel the Spirit bubble up, and the power of its passion, creativity, and vitality scares us.

Today, say, "Today I will listen to the wind. I will find the Spirit where she is."

Day 2
A Word from Uncle Wayne:
The fire does not consume.

The Burning Bush is a symbol of Spirit. The bush is ablaze, but not consumed. The Spirit is fire—passion, creativity, aflame in us. And we repress it!

Today, say, "I listen to my passions. I use the energy of my Spirit to bring new life."

Day 3
A Word from Uncle Wayne:
The Spirit speaks in strange language.

You know that little voice—the one that whispers, "Are you sure about that?" The one that proposes peace, not reprisal? Spirit sees others, sees their pain and confusion, and speaks words of comfort and understanding.

Today, say, "I will listen to the small voice of stillness, and not argue."

Day 4
A Word from Uncle Wayne:
The Spirit is energy.

There really isn't a *Spirit,* per se—there *is* universal energy pulsing in you, in rhythm with the rest of creation. Your energy is yours, so spend time with it.

Exercise: Rub your hands briskly together. Move them 2 or 3 inches apart. Concentrate on the space between your hands. Feel energy. Feel Spirit.

Day 5
A Word from Uncle Wayne:
The Spirit brings healing.

Energy flows where attention goes. Today, feel energy in your body, and begin to direct it. You may need a teacher for this.

In the meantime, go back to the hand rub exercise again, and then lay your hands on your neck. See what happens.

Day 6
A Word from Uncle Wayne:
The Spirit recognizes itself.

Jung coined the term *synchronicity* to describe meaningful coincidences—which are a gift of Spirit.

Today, say, "Nothing is a coincidence. I *know* this."

Day 7
A Word from Uncle Wayne:
Energy is the power of creation.

Spirit animates us—strong Spirit, powerful life. No question.

Today, tell your Spirit, "From now on, I will nurture you like a flame, and will allow you to grow. I will listen to you first. I will walk as you direct."

Love and Your Heart—Week 30

No mush here. The heart region of your body is the seat of your emotions, and especially is the home of the "feeling" of love.

This week, I would like to suggest that you get your heart under control. A rampant heart without mind and Spirit engaged *and* operating means trouble, every time.

Love is misunderstood. Typically, people experience love as *falling in love*. That form of love is hormonal.

Hormones seem to have a mind of their own, many become attracted to precisely the person who will "be trouble," once the effects of the hormones wear off.

The heart is the seat of *real* (and thus mostly non-hormonal) love. Real love involves the three realms equally—heart, mind and Spirit.

Scott Peck (*The Road Less Traveled*) suggested that there were three reasons to get married.

1) to have kids.
2) for the tension and conflict—he saw tension as the stimulus for keeping growing edges stimulated.
3) the most significant reason is to participate in the Spiritual growth of another person. This is the essence of real love.

Real love is openness to being of service. For example, you are drawn to people you can teach, and to people who can teach you. The recognition, the bond, is unmistakable. There is such a relief in knowing and being known in this sharing and love that *energy* flows.

Heart love is about full openness and intimate, deep sharing. It is about celebrating the success of your friend. It is not about manipulation. It is love for the sake of others.

※

What would we find, in your heart?

In what ways have you "hardened your heart?" In what ways are you open-hearted?

Day 1
A Word from Uncle Wayne:
Love is a process of unfolding.

Whom do you love? How did the relationship start? What is it based upon? Where is the relationship going?

Day 2
A Word from Uncle Wayne:
"My one, true love" is a myth.

As you walk through life, you will find people whom you love—you will feel romantic love, sexual love.

As your walk becomes proficient, you will meet your teachers and your students, and the love will be *agape* love—self-sharing and self-giving love—a participation in the other person's Spiritual growth.

Who are you in an *agape* relationship with?

Day 3
A Word from Uncle Wayne:
True lovers walk parallel paths.

Everyone is on a solo trip through life. Others are there to share with, talk with, receive directions from, but it is *our* walk. We have to move our feet, sort the data, and make choices.

It is good to find people on parallel paths, as it is fun to walk alongside another (or several others). Who is (are) your path partner(s)?

Day 4
A Word from Uncle Wayne:
The second you insist that another *change*, love goes away.

No one knows what *another* needs to learn, or from whom, or how. Your way is your way. While your way might provide a hint or guide for others, they need to find their own way, as you do.

Think about the people you love. Say, "Today, I choose to walk *with* you, hearing your questions, encouraging you to find your answers, but not attempting to live your life for you."

Day 5
A Word from Uncle Wayne:
Love yourself first.

True love is *not* selfless. Sacrificing yourself for someone else is stupid. You are responsible for *you* and *your* walk. From that place of taking care of yourself, you have energy to be of service.

It's like the flight attendant's admonition: "First put on your oxygen mask, then help others."

Remember that. Say, "I am like a battery. I can't serve others without being "charged up" myself."

Day 6
A Word from Uncle Wayne:
Feel your feelings, and then choose.

No sense criticizing yourself for your feelings. People on parallel paths often feel very strongly about each other.

They may decide that there needs to be sensual or sexual contact. Maybe. Maybe not.

It is not about hormones running rampant. It *is* about this: "Will acting out my passion help or hinder my walk, my friend's walk?"

Any of this familiar?

Day 7
A Word from Uncle Wayne:
Make contact.

Having said all of this, people on parallel paths *will* be physically connected.

Through discussion, set contact parameters. Then reach out. Touch. Support. Care. Encourage. What does not manipulate, heals.

Faith—Week 31

Faith, by its very nature, is faith *in* something. Yet, most people have faith *about* something. There is a profound difference here.

About implies description. Most people can describe what they have faith about, but are unable to demonstrate *how* they enact their faith.

More problematic, such people seem to be stuck with a list of rules they picked up from somewhere, which they then try to force others to follow.

True faith is not so much an intellectual agreement as it is a felt sense. Faith is a deep knowing that has very little to do with proof.

People of faith are *people of wisdom.* A wise person does **not** believe that there is something *outside* of them that has all their answers. Wisdom is recognizing that each of us has our own answers.

True faith is *faith in ourselves.* Because this makes us *self-responsible,* many run from this idea, as they think it is far better to have others (or some god) to blame.

The wise person understands that life simply *is.* There is not necessarily a reason for everything; there may not be a reason for *anything.* The wise person is content despite the ambiguity of life.

The wise person learns from life. If there is a purpose, it is *that we learn to be adults.* That we become mature. That we gain Mastery.

What do you have faith in?

Day 1
A Word from Uncle Wayne:
Imagine! You were given a life. Now, you are expected to actually live it.

You are the sum of your talents, minus the talents you block yourself from using.

List your talents in one column, and the ways you block yourself in another.

Day 2
A Word from Uncle Wayne:
Life is a classroom.

I do believe that we are here to learn. I do not believe that bad things happen to *test* us. (Such thinking makes World War II concentration camps hard to explain.)

What lesson seems to be the one you have to learn, again and again?

Day 3
A Word from Uncle Wayne:
The wise person learns lessons *the first time.*

One of the marks of wisdom is the ability to see what is happening, and then to make corrections.

We all fail. The wise person simply dusts herself off, gets up, and changes direction, with no blame.

How many times have you corrected your course on the first try? List examples.

Day 4
A Word from Uncle Wayne:
Wisdom / faith does not create "no problems."

How often have you heard someone say, "Boy, he must have really done something wrong for this to happen." Phooey. Things happen. The mark of wisdom is in the recovery.

How do *you* recover?

Day 5
A Word from Uncle Wayne:
Find your faith.

Faith is internal, and is reached through meditation and focus. Faith is a felt sense of peace, understanding, and contentment.

Find quiet time today, go inside, and find the place in your body where you feel your internal wisdom. Stay there for a bit.

Day 6
A Word from Uncle Wayne:
Remind yourself: you are nothing special.

Many play the game of "Why is this happening to *me*?" As in, "The world should treat me as if I were someone special."

You aren't. No one is.

Today, resolve to do "nobody special training." (With thanks to Ram Dass for this idea!)

Day 7
A Word from Uncle Wayne:
Gaining wisdom is enough.

Let us get real here. Decide, today, what will mark success for you. Money? Possessions? Power? Prestige? All are dust. Sand.

Reset your goals. Pick something that lasts. Pick wisdom.

Fear—Week 32

Fear is faith's opposite. Fear is the belief that we are victims. Fear comes from thinking other people can hurt you. Fear comes from thinking that external events can damage you.

Fear is a *choice*. Fear is not real, nor even particularly sensible.

Fear fades when confronted head on. *Action* defeats fear, as does a refusal to place blame.

Fear feeds upon itself, so its removal requires eliminating its root cause. We do this by rejecting victimizing ourselves, and we do that through self-responsibility.

If I do something wrong, I am response - *able*. I am able to respond by making amends, changes. If others wrongly blame me, I am response - *able*. I can refuse to play the blame game. I can refuse to get angry or get even. I can simply walk away. Leave.

The fearful person runs from self-responsibility, always in predictable ways—blame, hitting back, making excuses. And nothing changes. When you feel fear, then, ask, "Is this feeling appropriate or useful?"

Sometimes (rarely), it is—when you are threatened with physical assault, your fear triggers "fight or flight." Otherwise, all fear accomplishes is delaying a response by keeping you stuck.

Tell yourself, "*Now* is the time to take personal responsibility—I will respond."

What do you do, when fearful?

Day 1
A Word from Uncle Wayne:
"The only thing we have to fear is fear itself."
Franklin Delano Roosevelt

Fear feeds on itself.

What are the things you fear? What are they about?

Day 2
A Word from Uncle Wayne:
Fear blocks wisdom.

Wisdom seeks solutions. Fear seeks nothing but more fear. No matter how scary it seems, the next step is always to *take* the next step.

Meditate on what might be a next step, for you.

Day 3
A Word from Uncle Wayne:
Fear makes victims.

We are living in the Era of the Victim. Everyone is looking for someone to blame for his or her fear, his or her pain, and his or her failures. As we become *mature*, however, we have to give up victim-think. Victims wait for rescuers. The wise become response - able, and create change.

When do you feel like a victim? How old are you again?

Day 4
A Word from Uncle Wayne:
Fear makes us deaf and blind.

Fear draws us inward, to our internal theatre, where the fear plays with us, and cuts us off from the world. In that moment, we become helpless.

Think of a time when you were so tuned into your fear that you missed what was happening in the "real" (the physical) world. Today, vow to stay tuned in.

Day 5
A Word from Uncle Wayne:
Light defeats fear.

The light of knowledge, understanding, and wisdom defeats fear, every time. Light (enlightenment) comes to those who seek it.

Today, list three people farther along the path than you, whom you would trust to help you when you are fearful. Ask them if they will do that for you.

Day 6
A Word from Uncle Wayne:
Wisdom defeats fear, using "Aikido of the mind."

If you have ever watched an Aikido Master, you will notice that she simply redirects that which comes toward her. No matter what comes in, no matter how hard, the Master turns and redirects it.

No one controls you without your permission. (Memorize this!) See yourself, today, as someone who *deflects* attacks. Then try it. It works.

Day 7
A Word from Uncle Wayne:
Be of good cheer.

In the end, the mark of a wise soul is her or his ability to find joy and laughter amid difficulties. Seek the spring of joy that flows through you. Laugh a bit. Then, laugh some more. The fear will pass.

Good Behaviour—Week 33

How can we know what is good?

That may seem like a strange question. We all think we *should* know good from bad—right actions from wrong actions. The reality, as you are discovering, is that there are no hard and fast rules.

The more you progress along this path, the more ambiguity will exist. Why is this so?

Every rule ever created originally had a "good" reason behind it. It was a rule that *made sense*, given the times, the society, and the prevalent beliefs.

However, and this is important, rules must change as circumstances and understandings change.

The same idea applies to "good"—what was considered good in the past is not necessarily good now.

Think of slavery, for example. In the Southern US, slavery was considered not only "good," but also economically essential. Preachers of the day scoured the Bible to "prove" that even God approved of slavery.

Oddly, in some parts of the world, the underlying tenets of this skewed, race-based definition of what is "right and good" continue today.

Most uses of the word good" are quite arbitrary. When someone tries to force another to change their behaviour, the person will say, "It's for their own good." But is it?

For the purposes of this chapter, I'd propose that *good* is this: bringing peace, harmony, and light to oneself and to the world, without focussing on recognition or praise.

Doing *good* (good *behaviour*) is bringing elegance to all situations, and depth to all relationships, while taking responsibility for your walk, and yours alone.

※

How do you define what is good? Do you have a list of good and bad behaviours? Is it flexible, or fixed?

Can someone else be good, and yet follow a set of rules or principles that are different from yours?

Day 1
A Word from Uncle Wayne:
Good is as good *does.*

We are *not* good because we follow a list of rules. We enact goodness as we interact with the world and with ourselves.

But we sure have those lists, don't we? What is on your "good list?"

Day 2
A Word from Uncle Wayne:
Never settle for *"good enough."*

"Good enough" implies that a half-hearted effort is enough. In truth, there is "good" and "not good."

How often do you settle for "good enough?" Why?

Day 3
A Word from Uncle Wayne:
Good is sown in peace.

To treat ourselves, and the world, "good," we need to recognize that it is seldom about behaving ourselves. It's about asking, "What will bring peace and wholeness to this situation?"

What situation(s) in your life need(s) peace?

Day 4
A Word from Uncle Wayne:
A good person is responsible.

The hardest lesson is the responsibility lesson. I am not responsible for another soul on this planet. I cannot save anyone, do their learning for him or her, or "make them change." I am not to blame if they do not get it. What I am is *self*-responsible. I can choose how *I* respond. I can choose to respond out of love, peace, and goodness.

Questions?

Day 5
A Word from Uncle Wayne:
The question is, how do we "act" in the world?

The world is a neutral classroom where we discover who we are. We have endless opportunities to experiment.

The first thing to experiment with is your "good list." Why are things on this list? Why not other things? How do *you* decide?

Day 6
A Word from Uncle Wayne:
Good Humour is more than an ice cream bar.

To be at peace is to master the Buddha smile—the smile of infinite compassion.

Life simply is. We choose how we interpret it. Seeing life as good, having joy in our hearts, is paradise on earth. What does good humour mean to you?

Day 7
A Word from Uncle Wayne:
You are good.

Do you think you are not good enough? Do you imagine that you have problems? Are you constantly thinking that people are out to get you?

GET OVER IT!! Today, make a concerted effort to be at peace with those around you, and primarily with yourself.

Bad Behaviour—Week 34

As the theory of Yin and Yang explains, everything is mirrored by, and contains, its opposite. As there is good, so must there be bad. The only way we can *know* a thing, like good, is to recognize its opposite.

Some people inclined toward bad behaviour—as some are inclined toward good. The vast majority of people waffle back and forth, doing whatever occurs to them. They are brain dead, but not necessarily evil.

How to confront bad behaviour: Do not turn your back. Watch. Stay awake. By this, I mean, be aware of the intent of the behaviour.

It is true that some people may intend to hurt us. Now, of course, others can hurt us physically. But that's not what this chapter is about.

IMPORTANT! Physical violence is never OK!

No one can hurt your mind, heart, or spirit. Others do what they do, and we hurt ourselves over it. This is the second most difficult teaching there is. (Being self-responsible is the hardest.)

I'm talking about bad behaviour—the "games people play" in an attempt to "make us miserable."

People who intend us harm, misery, difficulty are actually operating out of fear, weakness, and powerlessness. It's up to us to learn their games, and to not pick up and stab ourselves with the knives they present.

What do you do, when confronting bad behaviour (aggression, criticism, manipulation)?

Day 1
A Word from Uncle Wayne:
Bad is as bad *does*.

All of us think "bad" thoughts. We cheerfully plot the death of our enemies. Then we jump all over ourselves, call ourselves names.

The only *real* bad behaviour is the bad behaviour we *enact*.

What do you *actually do* which might be considered bad? Short list?

Day 2
A Word from Uncle Wayne:
People who engage in bad behaviour are scared, powerless people.

Our typical reaction to confrontation and verbal aggression is fear, or escape. In my experience, learning to simply "watch" the other, without shutting down or backing away, negates the power of the attack.

And then you can see the other person's powerlessness.

Can you see impotence of such people?

Day 3
A Word from Uncle Wayne:
Bad behaviour is an attempt to trick others into saving you.

A client once told me it was my job to keep her alive. I was to be responsible for her. She decided that my role was to look after her, to decide for her.

I refused. I did agree to be the best therapist I could be. What she chose to do with her life was up to her.

Who do you try to make responsible for your life?

Day 4
A Word from Uncle Wayne:
Bad behaviour happens in the dark.

So, shine light. Be willing to stand firm, to admit your mistakes, but be resolute that you will not cut and run. People who play manipulative games are looking for unprotected backs. Confronted, they back away.

What do you need to confront, gently, yet firmly?

Day 5
A Word from Uncle Wayne:
Do not judge.

Bad simply *is*. Good simply is. The same action can be either good or bad, depending on *intent*.

What items do you put on the "bad behaviour, evil" list? Why are they there?

Day 6
A Word from Uncle Wayne:
Bad behaviour is removed with surgical precision, not hand grenades.

Often, when confronted with bad behaviour, we react by getting angry, feeling sorry for ourselves, or feeling abused. Then, we might take our emotion out on someone else—not the perpetrator.

You must deal with the situation you confront, and no other.

Think about your approach when confronting bad behaviour. What do you do?

Day 7
A Word from Uncle Wayne:
Be compassionate.

A compassionate *mindset* is what is important. If someone intends to harm you, and you cheerfully plot his or her demise, you are entering into his or her headspace. In the process, you become what you hate.

If you hold your enemy (in your head and heart) in a gentle way, nothing may change, but you will not have joined them in their cesspool. This is difficult, but worth the discipline.

Darkness—Week 35

There is something pervasive about darkness. In science, darkness is defined as "the absence of light." Where "bad" might refer to an act, to a person, or to a specific time or situation, darkness refers to the absence of an *alternative*.

Depression is often thought of as "darkness." A major, life-threatening spiritual crisis is called the "dark night of the soul." Without light, there is nothing. Shadow upon shadow.

Yet, in order to regain the light, one must embrace the darkness. (You have probably noticed by now that many of the themes thus far have been in "paradoxical couplets." That is intentional. Most Westerners think in terms of "either / or." It would be nice if life were that simple. As you have been seeing, however, in each "negative" is something positive, and in each "positive" is something negative. And a whole lot of grey in between.)

It is not enough simply to "bear" the darkness. You must "embrace" darkness. You must know darkness for what it is—and to *know* something, you have to experience it.

Most people, unfortunately, try to avoid the experience of embracing darkness.

To embrace darkness is to question darkness. To know what it fears.

The dark night of the soul often occurs when a person wants to move on in their understanding, but such a move requires a "leap of faith." This leap requires leaving behind, *permanently*, things you have held (perhaps all your life) to be true.

This is such a fearsome prospect that the person stops dead, and the darkness comes, and fear emerges.

If you face the darkness, it becomes a friend. It says, "Here is what I fear." Once spoken, the darkness dissipates.

❧❧❧

What happens, for you, as you confront darkness?

Day 1
A Word from Uncle Wayne:
Enter the darkness. Enter the night.

There is a pool of darkness within you, where you "stuff" the things you fear. The pool of darkness also contains "external" fears. External is in quotes because the fear actually exists in you—in how you see the world.

Make a list of the contents of your "pool of darkness."

Day 2
A Word from Uncle Wayne:
Die consciously.

Darkness *always* involves death. In order to move through darkness, the thing that is at the root of the blackness has to die—to be let go of—for good.

Look at your list. Pick an item. Submerge yourself in that one item. Feel it. Breathe it. Imagine letting it die.

Day 3
A Word from Uncle Wayne:
A Dark Night of the Soul seldom is.

One night, that is. Big-ticket items take time to work through. You shorten the process if you actually *start*.

Most people only *think* about starting, and then worry about how hard it will be, and then *stop*, without actually doing something.

Is this your pattern? If so, pick an item from your list, and start.

Day 4
A Word from Uncle Wayne:
It only takes a spark.

Think about the last few days. Have you made progress in your personal pool of darkness?

Each step seems small, but each is necessary as you walk your path. What was your first step, the next?

Day 5
A Word from Uncle Wayne:
It is always darkest just before dawn.

Recognize this. As we confront the things that are in our "pool of darkness," the issues loom larger, and we may feel worse. So, we shut down.

How often do you avoid pain, and thus miss "the cure?"

Day 6
A Word from Uncle Wayne:
What goes bump in *your* night?

In the dark, every "clunk" seems important. But have you noticed that we scare *ourselves* a whole lot more than something external does, or someone else does?

We scare ourselves by making situations worse than they are.

What things do you turn into nightmares? How?

Day 7
A Word from Uncle Wayne:
It is never dark when you know the territory.

Spend part of today blindfolded. Learn to see without your eyes. As you do, you will be amazed at what pops into your mind. This teaches you, sans blindfold, to "see" what is truly there, as opposed to what your imagination creates.

After all, no one has ever fallen down imaginary stairs. Many, however, have been so distracted by imaginary stairs that they have fallen down real ones.

Light—Week 36

Living in the light beats living in darkness, any day. Light (enlightenment) is what this book is all about.

Far too often, with our lack of discipline, we wander along in the dark, endlessly falling into the same holes, traps, pitfalls. Instead of choosing to see, we make excuses.

We enter into relationships with the same kind of person that got us into trouble the last time. Alternatively, we improve a bit, and find people we can "help," consigning ourselves to the role of cheerleader and nursemaid.

To be *light,* on the other hand, requires independence and focus. Light pushes back darkness precisely because it is not dependent upon anything else to "change," "go first," "be different," or "cooperate."

Light simply is. Light reveals things as they are. Light shows what is *real*. It does not rescue. It may mark the exit, but it does not force anyone to go that way.

This is hard. Most of us are on the path because we see the light and want more of it. We also figure those around us *should* want it too, so, we try to sell others on what we think we know.

We may be doing this because we want others' admiration. Or, perhaps we are trying to *help*. In *either* case, though, we have decided that the other person is on the wrong path and we know the *right* path.

To bring light is to say *nothing*. If what we know (if what you are learning) is correct, you should not need to prove it or demonstrate it. You simply *"be it."*

To learn takes commitment to the walk. It takes a humble nature and a willingness to be a *student* forever. To bring light, you have to surrender to the light.

What does "surrender to the light" mean to you?

Day 1
A Word from Uncle Wayne:
Surrender is *not* a four-letter word.

You cannot *own* enlightenment. It's a moment-by-moment process. You surrender to a way of *being*. The continual action of *surrendering* to the light is what opens us to moment-by-moment choice and presence.

Today, think, "surrender."

Day 2
A Word from Uncle Wayne:
Live your truth.

It is difficult to resist giving advice. As you learn more about *yourself*, you will notice an increase in your ability to "read" others. It is only natural to think that others are *interested* in what you have to say about them.

Here is a hint: *they're not!* Don't describe. Don't lecture or offer advice. Show enlightened living by being it!

Day 3
A Word from Uncle Wayne:
Wake up and pay attention!

To live in the light is to live in the here and now. Not only do you pay attention to your surroundings, but equally to your internal response *to* your surroundings.

If you spend too much time focussing on your internal theatre, a bus will hit you. Too much focus on what is around you, and you "miss" yourself.

Spend the day watching all of *you*. See what you learn.

Day 4
A Word from Uncle Wayne:
Bask in the glow.

If you choose to notice, walking in the light is, well, enlightening. (I did try to resist. Really!) But as we mentioned yesterday, you have to make an effort to pay attention.

Today, focus on the *feeling* of watching you watching you. Simply enjoy paying attention.

Day 5
A Word from Uncle Wayne:
Light, right? So, write about light.

Today, spend some time thinking about the most interesting thing you noticed in the last few days. Write it out in story form. Then, tell someone the story, *without interpretation*, sometime soon.

Day 6
A Word from Uncle Wayne:
"Come on, baby, light my fire."
(The Doors)

Go light a bonfire or fireplace fire somewhere, at night. Avoid using "starters" like charcoal lighter. Watch. Notice that fire gradually *pushes* the darkness back.

You can even see this "push back" effect when you turn on an incandescent light. Light is patient.

What would it be like for you, to bring light *slowly*?

Day 7
A Word from Uncle Wayne:
Light is not heavy, because it's light.

Have a non-serious day. As in, do not take the day, or you, very seriously. Look deep and find the humour. It is always there.

The Middle Way—Week 37

Not to endlessly belabour martial arts analogies, but balance and "The Middle Way" are sisters.

Martial arts are all about learning to be in balance. Before anything else, (and especially in the "soft" martial arts, like Tai Chi, Judo, Aikido, etc.) you must learn to find your balance.

To be in balance is to find the stable point between two or more forces, each of which pulls you in opposite directions.

The Buddhist Middle Path, or Middle Way, focusses on the balance point between opposites—or better, a way that encompasses and incorporates both.

The Yin / Yang symbol shows this unique way of seeing. There is an equal measure of black and white, light / dark, hot /cold, etc. But within the black is white. Within the white is black.

The Middle Way acknowledges this. For example, no matter how bad a person seems, there is also good within them. No matter how dark and bleak a situation, there is always a glimmer of light. In the midst of confusion, there is always clarity. If we look.

And that is the key. We tend to head in one direction only. We choose a way of seeing and give everything to defending that way, even if this leads us *away* from happiness, truth, and clarity.

If, on the other hand, we remember the rule of the Middle Way, we have a choice. Actually, we have many choices. We can reflect on each situation as it occurs and create a multitude of options.

The Middle Way says, "Perhaps." A situation seems good. Perhaps. A situation seems bad. Perhaps. Many times, major upheavals are actually great blessings.

To walk the Middle Way requires giving up the need to be right. You simply choose to find *your* peace, light, and truth.

What would The Middle Way be, for you?

Day 1
A Word from Uncle Wayne:
Focus on your middle.

In martial arts, balance and power come from the *hara*—Japanese for the lower belly. The Chinese call the centre of the hara the *Lower Dan Tien*. The same spot is also called the 2nd Chakra, and is located two inches below your navel.

Today, turn your attention there. See if you can feel this energy point.

Day 2
A Word from Uncle Wayne:
Breathe from your middle.

Now that you know where the spot is, breathe each breath to there. If you need help, stuff your fist inside your pants, just over the spot. Breathe deeply, so your hand moves out. Bingo. Do this repeatedly today.

Day 3
A Word from Uncle Wayne:
Just how unbalanced are you?

Pay attention to your physical balance today. How steady on your feet are you? Do you stumble or trip? Start to tip over? Just notice, and remind yourself that you are firmly attached to the planet.

Day 4
A Word from Uncle Wayne:
How often do you say, "perhaps?"

Balance is the ability to hold two or more forces in your body at once, and to redirect them to cancel each other out. *Perhaps* is the mental equivalent of physical balance.

Today, look for times when you "just know" that you are right, and someone else is wrong. Stop, and say, internally, "*Perhaps* her point of view is valid, too." See how that sits with you.

Day 5
A Word from Uncle Wayne:
Imagine "no conflict."

What would happen if you allowed for the possibility of a *multitude* of answers to any question or issue? Perhaps you would not always get your way, but you do not care about that any more, right?

Spend the day examining your belief system. In each case, say, "What is another perspective on this?"

Day 6
A Word from Uncle Wayne:
The Middle Way is not about surrender.

So, what's the point of being in balance? It's *not* to listen to someone else and to arbitrarily shift your viewpoint. Moving from one position to another position is rigidity, not flexibility.

The goal is to understand that *everything* we believe is provisional, and that other viewpoints are available. In this, we find balance.

Take a breath, then pick an issue, and see how long you can hold two opposing ideas about it in your head, without judgement.

Day 7
A Word from Uncle Wayne:
The wise person knows nothing.

Remember, you cannot learn if you think you already know.

Today, think of yourself as "a being in process." All you know is provisional. Tomorrow, you will think differently. (This is actually the truth, but we deny it.)

The Reactive Mind—Week 38

In physics class, we learned, "For every action there is an equal and opposite reaction."

On the physical level, this principle holds true. If you push a ball, it rolls in the direction of the push. Seldom, if ever, does it come back at you. (Things are less predictable at the subatomic level, but I digress...)

Many people assume that life itself is simply a series of actions and reactions. Someone treats us a certain way, and we have "no choice" but to react as we have in the past. If someone pushes us, we push back. We hear a tone of voice and we are off to the races.

The term for this type of behaviour is "the reactive mind." It is a good description of what *does* happen.

The sub-conscious mind is sort of like an interactive file cabinet. Things we learn go into file folders, and (important!) we choose the label on the folder.

As an illustration, imagine the following scene. You say something to your father that is a bit "lippy." He replies, "Don't you take that tone with me, young lady," and wops you on the butt, sends you to your room, and tells you that you are a rotten kid.

How do you feel? Angry. Scared. Hurt. Rejected.

Now, what do you suppose happens when, some 30 years later, your boss says, "You sure messed that one up!" and her tone of voice is similar to dad's?

You whip into your mind's file room, find the appropriately labelled file, and *immediately* feel angry, scared, hurt, and rejected.

There's more. When the incident with your dad happened,

perhaps you sat in your room and yelled at your dad through the door. Today, your reactive mind, hearing the same tone of voice, also drags up *the old reaction*. You yell at your boss, because she "made you."

You can tell that your reactive mind is involved when you hear yourself defending your behaviour in absolutes. "*No one* has the right to talk to me like that. I did what *anyone* would do. People *always* treat me disrespectfully."

Does this fit for you? What things do you react to? How?

Day 1
A Word from Uncle Wayne:
Who jerks your knee?

Re-read the intro for this week, and then watch yourself for "knee-jerk reactions" to input from another.

Do you sigh when your spouse asks you a question? Does your back go up when someone challenges your ideas? Notice what your head says. Write it all down.

Day 2
A Word from Uncle Wayne:
Who pushes your buttons?

If you were honest yesterday, you wrote something like, "My husband criticized my cooking and he made me angry." Change this to, "My husband criticized my cooking and *I* made me angry." Then, one more fix. "My husband criticized my cooking and I *chose* to make myself angry."

Fix all of yours.

Day 3
A Word from Uncle Wayne:
It is my hand on the switch.

To change reactive behaviour, you must take responsibility for setting yourself off.

Reactive behaviour is not automatic. It is a habit. We all know that habits are "hard to break." To which we say, "As hard as you make it."

Today, as you *react*, say, "I just *chose* that."

Day 4
A Word from Uncle Wayne:
Reactions are defenses—triggered by your belief that your ego is being attacked.

Notice that your knee-jerk reactions are always connected to feeling hard done by.

Today, again pay attention to your reactions. Ask yourself, "How am I choosing to bruise my ego with this?"

Day 5
A Word from Uncle Wayne:
The second syllable in knee-*jerk* is accurate.

Today, see if you can pull up short of a reaction. Just before you "sigh," choose something else. This will require that you pay attention, but that is the game we're playing!

Day 6
A Word from Uncle Wayne:
Whatever sets you off likely does not.

A story: Whenever a certain guy spoke, my back went up, and I angered myself. I spent a couple of *years* working on why, as my reaction was way out of proportion.

I finally realized he sounded like the father of my first girlfriend, who used to beat her with the buckle end of a belt. Bingo. Wasn't the current guy at all.

What about you? What is *really* going on when you set yourself off?

Day 7
A Word from Uncle Wayne:
Whatever grudge you are holding onto is not worth it.

You have probably found at least one knee-jerk reaction you want to *keep*.

You think that, regarding this situation, you really *are* hard done by, and if you shift, you will be forever jerked around. The jerk who jerks you around (the jerk!) causes you to defend yourself, knee-jerkingly.

Phooey. Give it up. Let it go. Grow up. What are you giving power to *that* one for?

The Responsive Mind—Week 39

The responsive mind is the mind of maturity, wholeness, and enlightenment.

There is no *cause* for *any* behaviour. No one makes us do anything. No situation demands one specific reaction. There is nothing in our lives that "has" to be a certain way.

Now, the only way you can get this one is to discover that, in your head, there is a gap between stimulus and response. It is the gap between *perception* and *interpretation*.

Because nothing in your head is "real," the gap between stimulus and response means we have an opportunity to change the response. Admittedly, in the beginning, that time gap is very small, but you *can* widen it.

To do so, you will have to pay attention. Rather than starting small, let us start big. What reaction of yours gets you into the *most* trouble?

As an example, imagine that you get angry, and then say stupid things.

The solution? Choose. The next time you feel anger coming on (boom, it's there!) you stop yourself, and take one breath. As you breathe, you ask yourself, "What is the best choice for this situation?" And you begin to make a list of *responses.*

What you will discover, as you begin to play this game, is that there are *many* choices—many responses. You can actually pick one or more to try, and see if they get you different reactions or responses.

What you are looking for are behaviours that lead to what you actually want to accomplish. If the situation always gets worse when you, for example, react with anger, is that what you are trying to accomplish? If not, create some space, have a breath, think, and change your response.

※※※

Imagine your one big issue that you judge is unchangeable. See if you can find one alternative response.

Day 1
A Word from Uncle Wayne:
Unstick yourself.

This week's work is about letting go of your "biggies." What did you discover yesterday, regarding being stuck? What did you tell yourself? Take a breath. Now, what are you willing to do about the biggies?

Day 2
A Word from Uncle Wayne:
Widen the gap.

Yes indeed, there is a gap between stimulus and response. All it takes to widen the gap is the *will* to widen it.

Notice I keep saying, "Take a breath." That is actually one of the best ways of widening gaps. The stronger the attack, the longer one takes breaths.

The goal is to see that most things we judge to be "attacks" are not attacks in the first place. You accomplish this by not reacting as if they are, while responding with compassion and understanding.

Today, widen the gap, with a breath.

Day 3
A Word from Uncle Wayne:
Widen your repertoire.

Pick a leftover knee-jerk reaction. Write it down. Now, write 10 different ways you could respond. Put them in order, say, of elegance. Then, try them out.

Day 4
A Word from Uncle Wayne:
Narrow your focus.

Pay attention. Often, a knee-jerk reaction follows when you doze off and lose focus—you get surprised.

Today, stay tuned, and experiment with responding *differently*. Speak to someone you might normally ignore. Go to work by a different route.

Day 5
A Word from Uncle Wayne:
Never settle for lukewarm responsiveness.

Imagine that, from now on, you are on a mission to be *responsive*. Never settle for OK. Work toward "a little more elegant, day by day." Ask yourself, "Why do I do this thing this way? What else could I do?"

Day 6
A Word from Uncle Wayne:
Be unpredictable.

In a wise way, of course. Sameness is boring. Try stretching your standard behaviours. See what happens. Keep the good ones.

Day 7
A Word from Uncle Wayne:
Don't Worry.
Be Happy.
(Bobby McFerrin)

Now *there* is a change for you! Are you? Happy? Why are you choosing not to be? Here is the *real* biggie. No matter what, there is always a choice. Happiness is not coming *tomorrow*, when the bills are paid and you're retired. All you have is today. Remember—be happy today!

Control—Week 40

For the next six weeks, we will explore governing ourselves. We will move from this lesson, Control, to Mastery.

Control, then, is the first step toward Mastery.

We say, "Get yourself under control!" What we mean is, "Behave yourself. Stop being an idiot." In this context, control is a way to stop being childish.

Real control is much more than this. Control is being aware of, and governing, *all* of your life experiences.

It is emphatically not about controlling *others*.

The walk into wholeness is about assessing what is *not* working for us. Here's a story about that.

As a child, teen, and young adult, I had quite the temper, paired with a sarcastic mouth. At age 31, I decided to learn to control both my temper and my mouth, as an *initial* step on this walk.

Controlling myself was a practice in *discipline;* I began by stopping myself from expressing anger *at* people. Tough, very tough, as I was working on a 31-year-old behaviour.

Be clear about this—being in control is not "turning yourself off." It is not having a "stiff upper lip." It is all about exercising your will so that what you do reflects who you are.

To this day, I feel anger, and to this day, I re-choose to express it through hitting a body bag, shouting at trees, through writing, and by working it through with close friends.

Control extends to all functions.

For example, whole breathing is something I have mentioned more than once. It takes *control* to breathe properly, as you have to monitor how you breathe, and quell your urge to short circuit the process.

Control is an act of will designed to allow you to move toward wholeness. Without it, you surrender your life to the winds of fate.

How would you describe "control?"

Do you think of it as something that "makes you behave," or is it the kind of control that is beginning (or continuing) to help you change your way of being?

Day 1
A Word from Uncle Wayne:
Stop blaming autopilot!

Make a list of all of the things you think are *out* of your control. As I noted, prior to age 31, I *thought* I had no real control over my angry outbursts. I learned differently.

What things about you do you write off as things you cannot change?

Day 2
A Word from Uncle Wayne:
Control one thing.

I have a friend, Scout Cloud Lee, who tells the story of how her mother "pushes her buttons." (I'm sure she'd admit that she pushes her *own* buttons…)

She describes going inside, where she "disconnects the button." Then, as a test, *she asks her mom to try again.* This is how we gain control.

Pick one item from yesterday's list. How will you "get, then test, your control?"

Day 3
A Word from Uncle Wayne:
Get the joke!

Being in control is actually a laughing matter. We tie ourselves in knots as we find the discipline necessary to live our lives differently.

Today, notice as you hook yourself into a silly behaviour, notice your attempt to be "under control," and have a laugh about it. Relax.

Day 4
A Word from Uncle Wayne:
You are not a kite.

So, stop blowing in the wind.

When people know what your buttons are, it seems they then can jerk you around. Remember who is *really* jerking your string! Remind yourself that you do not "blow" anywhere without you *deciding* to go there. Pay attention!

Day 5
A Word from Uncle Wayne:
Control your pace.

Today, focus as you walk. Watch your pace. Notice your attention span. Alter something, preferably your speed of walking. Slow down, speed up, and be careful.

The goal is to recognize how to control your *body* as well as how often you are lost in your internal chatter.

Day 6
A Word from Uncle Wayne:
Go play with yourself.

Sit in a comfortable chair. Think of something that is exciting to you, that stirs your passion. Now, notice the energy in your body. With your mind only, direct the energy around your body. Move it to your toes, your fingers, and the top of your head. End with the energy in your lower abdomen. Isn't control *fun*?

Day 7
A Word from Uncle Wayne:
Control something else.

Find some other behaviour to tackle. Work at one a week, but keep after each of the ones you have been working on. Play with getting your behaviour under your conscious control. Remember: all that is necessary is being *aware* of what is happening. When you get off autopilot, much strange behaviour just goes away.

Rigidity—Week 41

For many people, rigidity is a way of life. It is not unusual for people to move only so far in their walk, and then to freeze. They solidify their understandings at that point, either because of outside pressure to conform, or because they just do not want to have to walk any more.

As with control, rigidity affects all areas of our being.

Mentally, rigid people allow their heads to turn to concrete. They assume they have nothing more to learn. Of course, few get away with this. Mostly, their inner voice kicks up a fuss, trying to thaw them out. Then, they have a choice. Deal with the situation by moving again, or climb into the Prozac bottle.

Physically, body rigidity comes from the disuse or misuse of the body. In one of my Tai Chi classes are a couple who exercise regularly and yet have absolutely no sense of their bodies. As they move into a position, I might say, "Don't lean." They are unaware that they *are* leaning, even after I point it out. Scary.

Sexual rigidity almost doesn't need describing. Many people freeze around sex. Their legs, literally or figuratively, snap shut. They feel that they are going as far as they can, when in truth they are shutting down because they fear their own sexuality.

Spiritual rigidity comes in many flavours, but always involves the idea that your belief system is right and all others are wrong. Thus, the fervent New Age believer is just as stuck as the fundamentalist or atheist is.

Overall, rigidity keeps you stuck where you are. Some find it enough to stand still and to shout to the rooftops, "See! Here I am! I have arrived and I know the truth!"

I, on the other hand, suggest continual movement, even if that means having to admit that I do not know anything for sure.

※※※

In what ways and areas are you rigid? Use the four categories (mental, physical, sexual, and spiritual) and describe your rigidities.

Day 1
A Word from Uncle Wayne:
You are what your body shows.

Back to the mirror today. Take off your clothes and stand in front of a full-length mirror. Wiggle your body around. Look for stiffness and feel for soreness. Usually, you can *see* your body's rigidities. What does your body tell you? How are you holding yourself in?

Day 2
A Word from Uncle Wayne:
A mind set in concrete is not a pretty sight.

Today, look inside your head. What ideas do you hold that you will never change?

Make a list of all the things you know "absolutely, for sure." Now, burn the list.

Day 3
A Word from Uncle Wayne:
Baby, it's warm down here!

Write down your *sexual* rigidities. What do you tell yourself about yourself as a sexual person? What are your rules, your "do's and taboos?" Where did they come from? How do they hold you back?

Day 4
A Word from Uncle Wayne:
It's only rigid until it isn't.

Today, a body exercise. Find a rigid muscle. Try your neck or back. Now, gently, tighten the muscle further. Hold it for a count of five, then relax. Do this three times. Now, relax and take five full breaths. Move the muscle. Has it loosened? Work on a couple more.

Day 5
A Word from Uncle Wayne:
Move it or lose it.

Think about your body, your mind, and your beliefs as areas that have become stuck. Imagine being able to give yourself a shake, and each thing, in turn, would loosen. Now, get up and give yourself a shake.

Day 6
A Word from Uncle Wayne:
"It ain't over 'til it's over."
(Yogi Berra)

Think about your body, your beliefs, and your sexuality. Explain to yourself again how "where you are" and "what you believe" makes sense, and will "*always* be true."

Then, have a good laugh over this. Make a pact with yourself to explore the possibility that you may still have something to learn.

Day 7
A Word from Uncle Wayne:
Nothing is *ever* for sure.

Today, tell yourself, and others, that you do not have a clue about much of anything. Make a game of it.

The truth is that all we have are provisional answers about stuff, and circumstances change our understandings. We get in trouble trying to keep things the same when situations change. We overcome this by never assuming we know anything for sure.

Flexibility—Week 42

To move past both control and rigidity requires flexibility. That is what this book is all about.

I want to direct your attention to those things that are getting in your way. Then, we will work toward learning ways of being that demonstrate that you have choice.

Because flexibility is all about choice.

Mentally, flexibility is the same as *lateral thinking*—there are many ways to view things. Everything in the world is only (and exactly) as we describe it to ourselves. That is why no two people ever see a situation the same way.

The rigid person argues for their viewpoint. The flexible person understands that there are many, many viewpoints. The viewpoint they hold now is the one they hold *now*. If they are wise, they recognize that most understandings will change.

Regarding matters *physical*, as our bodies become more and more flexible, we are able to do new things well and familiar things better. Chi, energy, keeps us healthy and whole—and flows much more easily through a relaxed and flexible body.

Sexual flexibility is the willingness to experiment—it's not about to your ability to place your heels behind your ears, although that is nice, too! Being able to play, innovate, and try new things brings energy to lovemaking.

Spiritually, flexibility seems heretical. Yet, no one knows everything about matters spiritual. All we have are human definitions, and things change. Far better to do away with the systems of thought that bog us down, and learn to relate directly with our Spirits.

List your flexibilities, again using the four categories (mental, physical, sexual, and spiritual.)

Day 1
A Word from Uncle Wayne:
Learn to go with the flow.

Yesterday, you once again played the "I don't know" game. Today, try on someone else's point of view. As you find yourself stating one of your fixed positions, state it, then say, "Of course, another way of looking at this is… "

Day 2
A Word from Uncle Wayne:
Flexibility *is* as flexibility *does*.

Find a local Tai Chi or Yoga class. Sign up for at least six weeks. Go.

Day 3
A Word from Uncle Wayne:
Have a talk with your Spirit.

Doesn't matter what you believe about this, or even if you believe nothing at all. Just for today, in your head (so no one arrests you!) tell your Spirit what is happening for you. Ask it to show you something interesting. Then look around and see what you see.

Day 4
A Word from Uncle Wayne:
Fantasy is good for you.

Write down a sexual fantasy. Think about a movie or book you have read, where something was a sexual turn on, but something you would *never* try. Write a story describing you doing whatever it is you would not do.

Day 5
A Word from Uncle Wayne:
Live your fantasies.

Knew it was coming, didn't you? Go to yesterday's story. Figure out a way to make it happen. Be safe, but have fun.

If you are stuck, pick up a book called *Come Play With Me*. The book contains safe, fun fantasies to try.

Day 6
A Word from Uncle Wayne:
Feel yourself freeing up.

Today, walk around and notice your body. Stretch your spine, stand tall, shoulders comfortably back. Look straight ahead. Look people straight in the eye. Notice how free your body feels.

Day 7
A Word from Uncle Wayne:
Lose a few opinions.

Today, work on *not* expressing your opinion. Just listen to others and ask them how *they* see things. Find out how others make decisions, or why they hold the view they hold. You *may not* mention your own views. Tough, eh?

Balance—Week 43

Flexibility leads to balance, and not only in Tai Chi or the martial arts.

Mostly, as we learn or experience new things, we end up being like kids in a candy store. We want to stuff ourselves, and end up sick and miserable.

Balance is the art of "just enough."

Mentally, it is the balance between thinking and enjoying. Many people take this walk so *seriously*. They take more and more courses, read more and more books. All of which is OK, provided that you are allowing fun into your life. Laughing. Playing. Running and jumping. You know, fun.

Physically, it is the balance between pushing your body and resting your body. Both are necessary.

Sexually, it is the balance between ecstatic highs and the simple hugs and caresses of an evening dedicated to light, loving touch.

Spiritually, there is the fire and passion of actively working for the good of all, (may all sentient beings be happy…) and the joy that comes from watching a sunset while listening to "Amazing Grace." (Thanks, Haven!)

Balance comes almost naturally, if you pay attention. It comes from flexibility and an open mind, heart and Spirit.

What does balance mean for you? Are you "well balanced?" How?

Day 1
A Word from Uncle Wayne:
Your life is in the balance.

Indeed. The opposite is "out of balance," as in what happens when you stumble and are ready to fall. Review each of the four areas, and look for balances and imbalances. List them.

Day 2
A Word from Uncle Wayne:
Balance is all about groundedness.

In Tai Chi, you learn balance by constantly going back to structure. Structure has to do with how you orient your body, and how you attach it to the earth. Groundedness is the sense of being rooted to the earth.

Today, focus on your body. Does it feel rooted and grounded? Or, are you ready to blow over?

Day 3
A Word from Uncle Wayne:
Balanced emotions require a *range* of emotions.

Being balanced does not mean being stuck in neutral. It means being able to draw on a wide range of emotions, *and* using all of them. Productively. To be out of balance is to focus exclusively, or almost exclusively, on one type or group of emotions.

Write about your emotional *balance*.

Day 4
A Word from Uncle Wayne:
You may not need that trapeze in the bedroom.

A balanced sexual life is a conscious effort. Many men, for example, equate their sexuality with intercourse. Women often work toward intimacy first, semi-mindless sex second. Both are appropriate.

Think about what your sexual framework is. What is important? What are you neglecting? Find a partner and work on the neglected side.

Day 5
A Word from Uncle Wayne:
Find your roots.

If you took the suggestion seriously about doing Tai Chi or Yoga, go see your instructor. Have her or him look at your structure, groundedness, and balance. Ask for advice on being more in balance.

Day 6
A Word from Uncle Wayne:
A little peace is a good thing.

When was the last time you simply sat in silence and reflected on the beauty and symmetry of life? Make that today's goal. Pause, be silent, and notice the world as it passes by, unaided by you.

Day 7
A Word from Uncle Wayne:
Have a Spirit walk.

Spend time on a contemplative walk-about. Ask, "Who am I to be in the world, right now? How should I enact my gifts?" Listen for or look for your answers.

Flow—Week 44

The word *flow* has gradually worked its way into our vocabulary, and means pretty much the same as "being in the zone." This sports analogy describes a harmony of mind, body, and spirit that allows for smooth and elegant action, seemingly without thought or effort.

As to ordinary mortals who are in the *flow*: flow is impossible to describe with precision, but clearly is a state that virtually everyone has experienced at least once. Major characteristics of flow are the expansion of time, clarity of thought, and the ability to focus solely and deeply on the task before you.

When we *flow*, we are so engrossed in our work that time passes without notice. There are no distractions, despite people and events all around us. Pieces of the puzzle we are working on fall effortlessly into place. The result is as close to perfection as is humanly possible.

For most people, *flow* happens sporadically, and seemingly by chance.

I think that *flow* is our natural state of being, as opposed to the tuned out, distracted, underachiever state that most choose to exist in.

The question is not *whether* we can achieve flow. The question is why we resist it. All that is necessary to enter the flow is to give yourself conscious permission, and then to bring your attention to being quiet and focused.

Flow is a natural state. It is balanced and it is powerful. What can you do to "enter the flow" more often?

Day 1
A Word from Uncle Wayne:
To flow, let go.

While flow is a natural state, you cannot *force* it. If you try to *make* yourself enter the flow, you will be frustrated.

Our society holds onto the illusion that we *make* things happen. We create this illusion to give ourselves a false sense of control over our lives.

Today, notice how you structure your life. What do you think you are totally in control of?

Day 2
A Word from Uncle Wayne:
Letting go is not giving in.

There is a myth that if you let go, things will get out of hand. Actually, letting go is getting things out of *head*.

As soon as we assume that we can *solve* the issue we are confronting, we begin to intellectualize in predictable ways.

This is the opposite of being in the flow, where we look at our issue from *multiple* viewpoints. What are your myths about the consequences of letting go?

Day 3
A Word from Uncle Wayne:
Bring your attention back to the flow.

Today, create an image for being in the flow. Begin by taking fifteen minutes to remember a vivid flow experience. Your goal is to relive it, feelings and all.

Now, while holding on to the feeling, simply pose the question, "What is my symbol for this experience?"

Day 4
A Word from Uncle Wayne:
Test the flow.

Now that you have a symbol or metaphor, it is time to make use of it. Pick a project or task that you need to work on today. Hold an image of the project in your mind. Now, trigger your flow image. Be still. Watch and listen. See what emerges.

Day 5
A Word from Uncle Wayne:
Expand your experience.

Most of us think that *flow* is limited. For instance, some of us experience flow in our favourite sport, but seemingly not at work. Others experience it with projects, but not in relationships.

Today, begin to visualize flow happening in other situations and relationships.

Day 6
A Word from Uncle Wayne:
Seek flow challenges.

I distract myself when I hear loud voices. But rather than tighten up when I hear one, I choose to enter the flow. I still hear the voice, but I don't care, as I'm "into" what I'm actually doing.

What are your challenging situations? How can you "flow" around them?

Day 7
A Word from Uncle Wayne:
Never settle for less than you can be.

As we work together, we seek to find your limits, then push them a bit. Gently. With joy. With curiosity. Today, be kind to yourself. Enter the flow for the joy of it, and see how the world looks.

Mastery—Week 45

Mastery is both the final step, and the first step. The Master reaches a place of some understanding of self and the ways of enlightened living. Then, the fun starts.

In Zen archery, one sign of Mastery is that the archer can look at the target, look away, draw the bow, and shoot dead centre, without aiming. At later stages, it would appear that even the brief look is not necessary.

There is a Zen story about a guy who went to a Zen archery Master and studied faithfully. The student really applied himself, and learned the long bow. It was time for the big test. He looked at the target, looked away, began proper breathing, and drew the bow. The instant before he shot, his Master asked him a question.

The student was totally distracted, and un-drew the bow. He answered the question, calmed himself, and tried again. He could not draw the bow.

He got angry with his Master. His Master laughed and said, "I know that you mastered the *technique* weeks ago. The question is, 'Have you mastered *yourself?*'"

Mastery is the luxury of knowing that the lessons you have learned are *yours*. You know them, you live them, *and* you use them.

And then, you begin again.

Because you soon recognize that, in some areas, you are *still* distracted. In others, you are over-confident. The Master recognizes this, and turns his attention to the perfection of what still needs work.

Most of us have mastered one or two things, usually connected to work, or a beloved hobby. For example, many expert computer programmers easily drop into the zone and solve complex problems in their heads, writing elegant code in the process. They have mastered one thing, but still do not possess Mastery.

True Mastery is Mastery of the *self*—of the way that we *are* in the world. It is a goal, and precious few reach it. We know their names.

※※※

What things have you mastered? What will you *give* to master yourself?

Day 1
A Word from Uncle Wayne:
There is always a price to pay.

I cannot count the number of people I have worked with who said, "I should just *know* this stuff. I must be stupid!" They said this because everything I said to them, they'd heard before.

It is not whether you *know* it. The question is, "Will you pay the price necessary to *be* it?"

Day 2
A Word from Uncle Wayne:
Mastery is not another technique.

Mastery is a way of life, a way of being. As such, it is a continual choice. There is no "Now I've got it," because the cosmos loves to remind us how much we have left to learn. As soon as we master one thing, another thing arises within us.

Are you prepared to pay the price of *continual* learning?

Day 3
A Word from Uncle Wayne:
Mastery produces centeredness.

Mastery brings us fully into ourselves. The *things* we master are unimportant. They are equivalent to learning multiplication tables. We learn them not to learn them, but to teach us how to conceptualize math. Mastering activities teach us to understand ourselves.

So, who are you today? What are you still resisting?

Day 4
A Word from Uncle Wayne:
Self-knowledge is provisional.

The Master knows that the process of self-exploration is never over.

To settle for partial understanding or to attempt to *control* your life so that it is *predictable* is a short description of being dead and not knowing it.

Today, give yourself permission to know what you know, and to be curious about whom you will be next.

Day 5
A Word from Uncle Wayne:
The true Master, masters focus.

Focus is being in your body, being *aware*, and choosing to interact with others in a conscious and compassionate way. This is the freedom of being fully human.

Now, will you do choose to this all the time, while offering the same freedom to the people who are important to you?

Day 6
A Word from Uncle Wayne:
Master your body.

Think of one bad habit you have developed. What bodily disciplines are you avoiding that would counteract the habit?

Today, begin to master your bad habit.

Day 7
A Word from Uncle Wayne:
Be gentle with yourself, and with others.

Most Masters teach and live from a place of gentleness and humility. How does that sit with you?

The Archer's Bow—Week 46

Here is the conclusion to the story begun last week.

The archery student began again. He focused not on technique, but upon detached presence. He realized that anyone with basic skill could shoot the bow, but only the Master could *become* the bow.

The student archer realized that his *being* shoots the arrow; the bow simply provides the thrust.

It is never about the technique, the belief system, the religious group, or the political party. It is always about how the person uses the teaching, while employing the tools available.

The archer extends herself through the bow to empower the arrow, and to direct the arrow to the unseen target by the focus of her will.

It appears that the actual firing of the arrow is anticlimactic and almost unnecessary. Mastery is found in the preparation, the focus, the entry into flow, and the bringing together of muscle and mind as one draws the bow. At the point of release, the issue is already resolved.

The Master is able to walk away without looking at the target; so unimportant is the hitting of the centre. As such, Mastery is goalless.

Oh. The student became an accomplished Master, once he mastered both his *attention* and his *self*. Just for your information…

What would it be like to spend the rest of your life choosing to simply to observe yourself as you engage life, without setting up a system to *judge* your performance? (You choose nothing less than excellent results, of course, but that is not the *goal.* Get it?)

Day 1
A Word from Uncle Wayne:
How is always secondary to who.

Techniques are like paintbrushes. We do not confuse the paintbrush with the artist. The painting isn't the goal or the end, either. The painting is simply a clue to the identity and reality of the artist. The next painting reveals more, but never all that there is to know.

Who are you, today, as you interact with the world?

Day 2
A Word from Uncle Wayne:
Draw the bow smoothly.

Archers draw Zen long bows carefully. First, they are powerful, but secondly are fragile. Learning to pull elegantly is the basis of Mastery.

Examine the things you do well. What would it be like to be more elegantly involved with the things you do?

Day 3
A Word from Uncle Wayne:
Open your eyes and see.

One of the dangers of Mastery is *complacency*. You can get so good at a thing that you can engage in the activity and not be there, *present*. This is not Mastery. This is laziness.

Today, think about the things you have mastered. Have you moved from Mastery to inattention?

Day 4
A Word from Uncle Wayne:
Tune in.

Mastery is about observing yourself as you live your life. In the past, you tuned out because you were unfocused. As you move in and out of Mastery, you may go "non-present" because your life has become more understandable.

Today, simply pay attention to your non-present moments.

※

Day 5
A Word from Uncle Wayne:
Nothing is unimportant.

Think about it. Why are you where you are now, with the people you are with? Coincidence? I think not. Be here, be aware, feel your feelings, and explore the mystery of "why now, why here?"

※

Day 6
A Word from Uncle Wayne:
Revisit the rough edges.

The archer had to rethink his approach to Mastery, precisely at the point when he had mastered drawing the bow.

The real work was gaining understanding of what it meant to be *himself*, engaged in being an archer. In the end, it was not about where the arrow landed. It was about his self-knowledge as he *also* was 'archer-ing.'

You are *not* what you do, but rather *how* you do you. You

are *you,* interacting with yourself and others through, among other things, your skill set. How does that sit with you?

Day 7
A Word from Uncle Wayne:
Get to know yourself. Again.

Write about who you are at this phase of your walk. What do you know? What are you curious about? What have you mastered? What has mastered you?

Patience – Making Tea—Week 47

I once worked with a client who thought he had a problem. He was making himself annoyed and anxious, as he wanted to do several things at once—he was frustrating himself, especially when it appeared that nothing was working out.

I suggested that he slow down, learn some new ways of doing things, and recognize what he had already accomplished.

He looked very impatient. He made it clear—he wanted to change, and he wanted to change *now*. He saw this as another project, one of many, and each was clamouring for completion. And nothing was completed.

Patience is necessary, because change, shifting, takes *time*. Now, you can shift anything immediately, but true change takes time to mature. You have to be willing to see the process through.

I suggest making tea.

Making tea is a way of taking a break from a situation. It is a *short* break, however, designed to redirect the momentum of resistance to change, to stop anger and resistance, and to get things back on track.

The process is simple. For example: when you are not communicating the way you want to, take a short break, a pause. Say, "Tea time." You then go to the kitchen and make tea.

You watch the water boil; watch the steam rise to the ceiling, as your steam rises with it. You make the tea, share it with your partner, drink it, and return to the discussion at hand.

Patience is encapsulated in the art of making tea. Learn to stop, to pause, to take a break. Allow matters to come to a rest. No change comes from excessive pressure—excessive pressure brings breakage.

How patient are you?

Day 1
A Word from Uncle Wayne:
It is far better to watch the steam rise than to boil yourself.

It is so that continually letting yourself become angry (it *is* a choice!) is life-threatening behaviour.

How many ways can you justify getting angry? Write them down.

Day 2
A Word from Uncle Wayne:
Patience is not weakness.

An interesting exercise is to watch a martial arts master size up an opponent, especially in the "soft" martial arts, like Aikido. For the longest time, the master may do nothing. Then, boom. Action, typically just enough to get the job done.

To be patient is to take the time to understand what is *really* happening. How do you stop yourself from being patient?

Day 3
A Word from Uncle Wayne:
"Begin with the end in mind."
(Steven Covey)

I can't believe how many times I heard a client say, "Every time I say (or do) that, she gets angry." I ask, "What result *did* you want?" He says, "I wanted her to change." I ask, "Did she?" He replies, "Nope."

I ask, "Then why do you keep doing something that gets you a result you don't want?" I have yet to hear a good answer to that question.

What is yours?

Day 4
A Word from Uncle Wayne:
Make *peace* your goal.

The book, *A Course in Miracles* puts it, "I could have peace instead of this."

No one wants to fight all the time, get angry, cause turmoil. However, drama continues to happen.

How do you keep your turmoil "happening?" What are some alternatives?

Day 5
A Word from Uncle Wayne:
Pause often; check in, for no particular reason.

To adopt a position of peace, to be patient, requires learning to pause.

In the midst of an emotion, today, just stop. It does not matter what emotion, just stop. Create quiet and see what happens. At the very least, you will have a break from yourself.

Day 6
A Word from Uncle Wayne:
Take a five-minute break.

Today, insert a few five-minute meditation breaks, and follow your breath in and out.

As we have said, breathing is a good way to stay alive. Nice, slow, deep breaths. Now. Often.

Day 7
A Word from Uncle Wayne:
Make a tea deal.

Make a deal with significant others. As the tension rises, one or the other of you will offer a tea break, followed by a calm return to the topic at hand.

How many people would you be willing to have such a deal with?

Destiny—Week 48

I do not like the common description of "having a *destiny*." Commonly, the word is defined:

1. The inevitable or necessary fate to which a particular person or thing is destined; one's lot.
2. A predetermined course of events considered as something beyond human power or control.
3. The power or agency thought to predetermine events: *Destiny brought them together.*
   www.thefreedictionary.com/destiny

Mostly, we use the word to describe a pre-ordained path people *must* walk. We hear that some people are "destined for greatness." Others disappear on their way to their destiny. Tragedy seems to attract destiny thinking—we lay most tragedies at "fate's door."

Destiny thinking is limiting. It presupposes that our walk is about finding the one *right* path. Once you find it, everything will work out. Of course, such thinking has a perfect track record, because if things *aren't* working out, obviously you missed your destiny.

So, learn *this* lesson. *There is no destiny.* There is just you, living out your life. Some choices you make are good, some are bad. The test to evaluate your life choices: are you getting results that benefit you and others?

Is there one right path, one right person, one right career? No. There are many. The question is, can you learn the lessons each choice brings?

Do you believe in destiny? Do you think there is only one "right choice?"

Day 1
A Word from Uncle Wayne:
Have "No destiny" as your destiny.

Today, think about when you were growing up, and all the people who told you what or whom you *should* be, when you grew up. List those "identities." Do any of them really fit? How so, or why not?

Day 2
A Word from Uncle Wayne:
You are *all* of you.

Make a list of everything anyone has told you about yourself that they found unacceptable. OK. Just the important ones.

Day 3
A Word from Uncle Wayne:
Who you are changes with each breath.

Your body and your thinking and your being change all the time, or you are dead. Get that one. Now, look at the last two lists. How often is your behaviour *today* dictated by the contents of these lists?

Day 4
A Word from Uncle Wayne:
There is no pre-determined bad or good.
There is just *life*.

Life happens. Often, what happens is due to the choices we make, but even then, most choices can have *several* outcomes. We learn from our outcomes, but really, all we learn is how something came out *that time.* Each situation is new. Remember that.

Day 5
A Word from Uncle Wayne:
"Bad" things are never punishments.

Believing that bad things are punishments is the result of destiny thinking. Instead, remember that what happens, happens.

The question is: What will you *do* with and learn from what happens? And how do you resist this idea?

Day 6
A Word from Uncle Wayne:
Live for today.

Tough, this. I was just speaking to a friend. She said that she expected a situation to clear up soon, and *then* she would be happy. In the meantime, it was her fate to be plagued with problems.

Do you ever think this way?

Day 7
A Word from Uncle Wayne:
Set yourself free.

Burn the lists from day one and two. Let go of the things people told you about yourself. Re-invent yourself, each morning.

Vocation—Week 49

Vocation is a term that came into public usage in the late 80s and 90s. Prior to this time, it was assumed that most 'regular people' had jobs or careers or professions, but 'the religious' (a term for ministers, priests, rabbis) had *vocations*.

In other words, 'normal' people went to work; the 'holy' worked for God.

Then, in the late 80s, it became apparent to many people that a vocational calling was not limited to 'the religious.'

Each of us is called to our own particular brand of service. How we enact this service is determined by the particular "skill set" we have. That skill set is "bred in our genes—our bones."

There is a vast array of skills (talents, gifts, abilities—you pick the word.) Yet, many people choose to live their lives in direct opposition to their skills and abilities—their vocation.

Our society expects eighteen-year-olds to figure out a career for themselves. I often wonder how many of us would go to an eighteen-year-old for advice of *any* sort. Yet we routinely expect young people to set themselves firmly on a course for the rest of their lives.

Some do what their parents did. Some choose to do *nothing* their parents did. Some choose a career based upon income. Some pick a thing they are interested in, maybe even drawn to.

A precious few *live* their vocation. The rest get bored, get complacent, and get stuck.

The idea of "calling" is apt. If you listen, you hear yourself being "called" to do something. Something different. Perhaps outrageous. You get a sense that you would derive pleasure from it, and the world would benefit. This is a vocation.

※※※

Is what you are doing your job or your vocation? What is your vocation? Don't know? Would you like to know?

Day 1
A Word from Uncle Wayne:
Listen to the voice within.

In practical terms, there is nothing startling or new about the vocation each of us is "called to." In fact, thinking about your vocation often produces the, "Oh, that again" reaction. Despite our reluctance, we are called into service, through the full use of our gifts.

What is that call, for you?

Day 2
A Word from Uncle Wayne:
Examine your life.

Are you content? Why not? What are you waiting for? What do you think needs to happen first, and *then* you'll be content? What would happen if you decided, first of all, simply to be content?

Day 3
A Word from Uncle Wayne:
"You gotta go where you want to go, do what you wanna do..."
(The Mamas & the Papas)

How many "what you are doing now" decisions were made by you years and years ago? Do you say, "Well, that's what I decided, and now I'm stuck with it?" Why?

Day 4
A Word from Uncle Wayne:
The picture is never complete.

We are works of art—works in progress. We learn about ourselves, and there is more to learn. We advance our skill set, and there is more to learn. We learn to communicate well, and there is more to learn.

Many people decide they will be content when they understand everything (get enlightened, whatever). Again, I ask, will you choose to be content right *now*?

Day 5
A Word from Uncle Wayne:
Imagine *living* your vocation.

Prepare yourself, by actively imagining your vocation. Maybe it is what you are doing now, but a more elegant version. Maybe it is a change in direction.

Whatever. Imagine it happening, now.

Day 6
A Word from Uncle Wayne:
Do your best, and enjoy the results.

Mostly, we judge our situation, or ourselves, and find some lack. I suspect that, even if things were *perfect* there would be a way to say, "Yeah, but just wait until tomorrow!"

Vocational thinking is the simple choice to do your best, with service in mind, and then to say, "Well done!" What would such a life be like, for you?

Day 7
A Word from Uncle Wayne:
Make yourself happen.

Do not put yourself off for another second. Everything you need to be whole is right here, right now. All you are required to do is to *act* as if this is true, by elegantly enacting what you know *now*. Then, learn more, practice, and do those things well, too.

Wholeness—Week 50

We come to the crux of your journey—wholeness. Let me begin with a stab at a definition:

"Wholeness is the state of being whereby a person knows herself intimately, manages her energy strategically, and lives out her vocation in harmony and in balance, within and without."

A little unpacking.

Intimate knowledge—in the beginning of our journey, we talked about the basics—knowing your body, your mind, your spirit, and your emotions.

Most of us, until we make the effort, simply feel and then react, much like an amoeba that gets poked. Intimate knowledge is an endless quest into ourselves. We learn how we motivate ourselves, drive ourselves, please ourselves, and annoy ourselves. We learn to be with ourselves, without criticism. We learn to be with others, without judgement. We especially learn to *choose* whom we allow into our circle of intimates.

Strategic energy management—we have discussed the use of energy. The energy within us is finite—we each have a certain amount to use. It is a renewable resource, through focus, meditation, but it also goes where the mind flows. Nothing eats up energy more thoroughly than unresolved conflicts or issues. The *whole* person has learned to identify and correct ill-used energy.

The energy we have (and make) powers our creativity, our physical vitality, our passion, and our physical expressions. Energy can best be directed by a whole person, much as the Zen Archer directs the arrow from bow to target.

We have spoken of *vocation*. We have examined its power as a way of being.

Harmony within and without was discussed, in terms of *balance* and *Mastery*. We have noted that there is both internal and external Mastery. Internally, we deal with our self-knowledge and progress only insofar as we forgive ourselves. Externally, we choose whom to align ourselves with as we live out our vocation.

How "whole" are you in the following areas: mental, physical, spiritual, sexual, in terms of creativity, in terms of the expression of your passion, in terms of living out your vocation?

Day 1
A Word from Uncle Wayne:
The whole is more than the sum of the parts.

Often, clients understand something about themselves, apply it, and feel better. Then, I'd suggest that what they learned, say, about creativity is *also* a lesson about their sexuality or spirituality. The argument begins.

The newly creative person *could* extend their learning to their souls. It's all the same lesson, unless you choose to break yourself into parts.

How fragmented are you?

Day 2
A Word from Uncle Wayne:
There is only one lesson.

Wholeness, as defined above, is all that there is. We may think that we need to approach this piece by piece, but that is because that is the way we have always done it. We stub our toe, and glare at what we stubbed it on. Never do we look at the *person who stubbed his toe.*

Today, remember that you only have one thing to work on, and that is "to be wholly yourself."

Day 3
A Word from Uncle Wayne:
Wholeness = Happiness.
Happiness = Wholeness.

Most people think happiness is around the corner, as opposed to their present state of being. They endlessly *wait* for "it" to happen. Same with wholeness—it seems that something is always missing.

Get over it! You are who you are *today*, and nothing is missing. Can you believe it? *Will* you believe it?

Day 4
A Word from Uncle Wayne:
Live now.

For many, it takes a wakeup call—illness, a death in the family, a job loss, or other large event to begin the process of self and life examination. Most conclude that they had been living life in *anticipation* of better things to come, and had missed days and months and years of their real life in the process.

How much "in the now" are you?

Day 5
A Word from Uncle Wayne:
Question everything.

That is what we have been doing in this book. Spend today asking yourself why you do what you do. Why do you believe that? What is real about what you just did? How do you decide?

Day 6
A Word from Uncle Wayne:
Trust in nothing outside of you.
Trust yourself to know.

Bring your focus back to *you* and be consistent with yourself. Depend on yourself—that you have your answers within you. What do you trust in?

Day 7
A Word from Uncle Wayne:
It is all about you.

Who did you think it was about? Come on, get over it. Today. There is just you. Take a breath. That is you, and that is it. Now, live!

Servanthood—Week 51

So, what lies beyond wholeness? Servanthood.

Scary word. Servanthood implies, indeed *demands,* surrender to someone or something. Mystics from many places and times have found this place of surrender.

What, exactly, might be expected of you?

One thing will be *commitment.* And that commitment will be expressed in your pledge to completely live out your wholeness, while at the same time surrendering the need to beat up on yourself when you fail to be "in charge," to be "special."

You will be expected to teach what you have learned. Others will be drawn to you, and you are obligated to gently bring them to their own point of surrender.

You will be obliged to continue your quest.

You will notice that this book loops around. Back to the beginning for you. On second reading, with new eyes, the concepts we have discussed will take on a new clarity. As long as you choose not to stop your walk.

The servant seeks the welfare of others first. The servant—serves. The servant brings nourishment to the hungry and water to the thirsty.

Are you ready to serve? To surrender? If not, how are you stopping yourself?

Day 1
A Word from Uncle Wayne:
"Be the change you want to see in the world."
(Gandhi... or not!)

Life is as it is. Surrender your need to change it. Now, that does not mean giving up. That means that you stop trying to change the world, and focus on *changing yourself.*

Focus on being yourself. Focus on becoming present in the world. Hunger, for example, is "solved" one person at a time, as you feed someone, not in wishing that there were no hunger. Get it?

Day 2
A Word from Uncle Wayne:
Give what is needed, not what is requested.

Those around you are likely trying to get you to make their lives easy for them, and you are responding by trying to get them to do it *your* way.

Stop. Encourage everyone around you to find his or her own answers. What would that be like, for you?

Day 3
A Word from Uncle Wayne:
Give yourself away.

The less you think you need, the more you have to give. Offer yourself to others, freely and without hooks. How does that feel?

Day 4
A Word from Uncle Wayne:
Surrender – to vocation – to your highest Self.

Likely, yesterday's idea brought up all kinds of "They'll take advantage of me" stuff. I would ask you to wonder how anyone could take advantage of you if you do not *let* them. It is your choice to give fully of who you are, to whom you choose.

What have you decided that your path of purpose is?

Day 5
A Word from Uncle Wayne:
Surrender the need to keep score.

Most people do, you know. Keep score. Sure, you will do this wholeness thing, just as long as no one makes any demands. Sure, you will be nice, but your spouse has to be nice first. Sure you will be kind to all those who are kind to you. Sure. Sound familiar?

Day 6
A Word from Uncle Wayne:
Surrender to your wholeness.

That is the key. You admit, in fear and trembling, that you are already whole, and in need of nothing. Right now. And then, you live from there, each day. Will you?

Day 7
A Word from Uncle Wayne:
You are who you are.

That is who you are. The whole package, warts and foibles and all. You are, wait for it... you. Surrender. To yourself.

Enlightenment—Week 52

The Buddha was once asked who he was—a god, a master, etc. He denied all of the labels, and replied, "I am awake."

This experience of awake-ness, this moment-by-moment awareness, is the beginning and end of being truly and completely human.

You are here for a reason—to walk your path of purpose. You are incarnated (made flesh—in a body) to live out your vocation through the power of wholeness.

When you are awake, you discover, elegantly and easily, your next step. What to do is right in front of you. However, you have to stay on your toes, with your eyes open.

A friend was distressing herself. She had been working frantically for weeks, trying to sort out her life, her direction, and also to find a place to live. Despairing, she called, and I offered to drive to her place to talk.

On the way, I was wondering what to say to my friend. I turned onto a busy highway. Ahead, on the shoulder, I saw a bike on its side. There was someone collapsed against the bike, hunched over. I thought, "Wow. That person must be hurt."

And the traffic was flying by at 80 km per hour. I readied myself to pull over. As I passed the bike, I glanced out the side window. The guy was sitting on the ground, using the bike seat as a backrest. He was reading a book!

I told my friend the story, and suggested she take a rest—in the midst of her mind's "traffic"—from her frantic flitting. It was the story she needed to hear.

Never doubt. Listen. And hear. Look, and see.

Day 1
A Word from Uncle Wayne:
It's all pretty simple.

So long as you don't make it complex. When we step away from pat answers and judgements of "right and wrong," life, and the next step, appears.

How can you get out of your own way?

Day 2
A Word from Uncle Wayne:
Enlightened is who we are.

It's not the possession, of "the special," or the blessed. The irony is that we all *are* it, and don't notice.

Think of all of the ways you hide the truth of yourself from yourself. List all of the ways you choose to miss what is right in front of you.

Day 3
A Word from Uncle Wayne:
Enlightenment demands all of you.

Don't settle for being aware *part* of the time. It's too confusing and draining. Make the commitment to *fully* wake up.

What are you afraid will happen if you devote all of your being and awareness to living while fully awake?

Day 4
A Word from Uncle Wayne:
Keep your eyes open. And your ears.

The answers you seek appear *mysteriously*, in conversation, on billboards, commercials, chance meetings, comments.

What? You thought you were going to get voicemail? Listen. Look. Today—every day, for the message you need.

Day 5
A Word from Uncle Wayne:
The messages are subtle and often presented with a wicked sense of humour.

Like my story for the week, the cosmos continually drops teachings in my lap, more often than not funny ones. If the lesson is painful, I know that I've been missing or ignoring something.

Listen. Look. See. Do you hear the cosmos laughing?

Day 6
A Word from Uncle Wayne:
Enlightenment is.

Being human in a physical universe causes everything we experience. It is what it is, despite our wishing for a magical, no pain existence. The vagaries of life give meaning to everything. Do you understand this?

Day 7
A Word from Uncle Wayne:
Our work is finished. So, start again.

Last day. We made it. Except, funny thing, we are here, as ourselves, yearning to learn, to be, to be *whole*. Now, we recognize that we *are* whole, and tomorrow, we will be even more whole, as we will be one day wiser.

And so, if you will, we begin again.

Rock

The rocks in your life are the things you now *choose* to believe in, regardless of what someone once told you.

They are *your* truths, and they will change and deepen as your wisdom deepens. Dig deep. Find rock. Be at peace. And begin the task again.

See you at the beginning.

Epilogue

Thanks for joining me on this journey. This book has evolved and changed as my thinking has changed, and now, in 2015, almost 20 years since it first appeared, another edit is finished.

When I release it, it will be a conditional work in progress, as am I, as are you.

This book provides not only a guide for you but also a tracing of the evolution of you own understandings about wholeness. Each day you learn again how little you know, despite all that you know.

I wish you well on your journey. And I'd love to hear your story. Our address is at the front of the book. Drop us a line.

Lovingly,

Wayne

Also by Wayne C. Allen:

Available from The Phoenix Centre Press

Books:

This Endless Moment

Worthwhile change comes at a price. If you're tired of the same old relationships, the same situations cropping up again and again, and you find yourself stuck in the middle, then right now, you can do something about it! It's time to decide!

If you are willing to commit to living the life you have dreamed of, surrounded by meaningful and deep relationships, while making a real difference in the world, you need *This Endless Moment*.

Half Asleep in the Buddha Hall

Wayne's "Eastern" book takes you by the hand and leads you to Zen-based peace of mind.

Half Asleep in the Buddha Hall is a Zen based guide to living life fully and deeply. Using Zen stories old and new, as well as other illustrations and exercises, Wayne C. Allen takes you on an adventure into the uncharted territory of yourself.

Find Your Perfect Partner

Back in 1999, Wayne wrote a booklet called "The List of 50." "The List" was a guide to help you decide who to be in relationship with.

Wayne expanded upon this concept of conscious dating, and turned it into a book.

In addition to completely revising the structure and contents of the booklet, Wayne has included comments from readers, as well as sample *Lists of 50*.

The. Best. Relationship. Ever.

The. Best. Relationship. Ever. is both a learning tool, and a step-by-step guide — a plan you will implement — to chart the new direction in your life and relationship.

As you read, you *will* discover:

- 8 reasons you've failed at relating — we examine what goes wrong

- 3 problems people have with communication — once you know what doesn't work, you're ready for what does!

- Sam and Sally, and learn how to really mess up a relationship! — you see their mis-steps, and learn from them.

- a brand new model for being in relationship. I call this *Elegant, Intimate Relating*.

- how "labelling" your partner gets in the way of *Elegant, Intimate Relating*. You'll see that *Elegant, Intimate Relating* means no judging and blaming.

- the rules and practice of dialogue. Each conversation is worthy of doing well!

- what to do, and when. You'll have the tools you need, right in front of you.

www.ingramcontent.com/pod-product-compliance
Lightning Source LLC
Chambersburg PA
CBHW070642160426
43194CB00009B/1546